Lost Ancient Technology Of Egypt

Copyright Brien Foerster 2014

Cover copyright Bryan Foerster 2014

Dedication

I dedicate this book to those that ignited my interest in ancient Egypt, and those that fuelled that interest into a passion that grows each day. First of all to my mother Ann, who read me bedtime stories of the lives of the pharaohs, classical Greece and Rome, and global mythology. To my dear wife Irene, who has accompanied me to the magical land, and supported me when I had to go alone. To those great scholars, Graham Hancock, Robert Bauval, John Anthony West, Christopher Dunn and Robert Schoch whose insights into ancient Egypt stirred up controversy and in some cases vehement attacks from conventional scholars.

I wish also to thank all of the Egyptologists whose work has revealed so much that we now know about the dynastic Egyptians; who they were, when they lived, and what they accomplished. But my deepest love and respect goes to Stephen Mehler, Yousef, Patricia and the rest of the Awyan family, who live across the street from the Giza Plateau. Their warmth of spirit, dedication to the true knowledge of the ancient land, and always open door has made each and every one of them a member of my family.

And finally, this book is especially dedicated to Abd'El Hakim Awyan, archaeologist, Egyptologist, traditional wisdom keeper and patriarch of the Awyan family. I often feel his presence when we are in the ancient sites, and sense him smiling as we all work together to unravel these mysteries of his beloved Khemit. He, along with Stephen Mehler created the study now known as Khemitology, which introduces into the pool of knowledge many aspects and interpretations which conventional Egyptology does not, or cannot address.

Hakim's knowledge and wisdom came from degrees in archaeology and Egyptology, but what made his approach to the history of Egypt unique is that he spent most of his life as a tour guide, and from childhood learned from his observations in the field, as well as consulting with those who were the caretakers of the sacred sites. This oral tradition has seemingly been ignored by most Egyptologists, and few are those, such as Hakim, who have been capable of acquiring a fuller history of this ancient land.

Forward

I was quite pleased when Brien Foerster asked me to write the forward for this book—pleased not only because Brien has become a respected colleague and good friend, but mainly because I consider him to be one of the clearest and best researchers of ancient cultures and civilizations in the world today.

My own interests and pursuits in the field of human prehistory and ancient history now approaches 50 years of research. My main area of interest has been the civilization known as ancient Egypt—an enduring interest since the age of eight—and became my main professional area since 1968. I must mention two profound teachers who have supremely guided me in this direction: the first being Professor Francois Bordes, former Director of Antiquities for SW France, one of the great prehistorians of the 20th Century. Prof. Bordes, whose doctorate was in geology, taught me not only basic field archaeology in the summer of 1974, but the fundamentals of geology—which I now consider essential for any archaeologist. But my greatest teacher appeared only when I was ready—and only after years of research on my own in academic Egyptology.

I became involved in the research of ancient crystal skulls in the 1980s, was featured in a book on the subject and was then on a panel at the San Francisco Whole Life Expo in 1987. There I met two people manning a booth for a travel agency—they were Dr. Ruth and Harry Hover, agents for Power Places Tours who led spiritual trips to Egypt. I became great friends with Ruth and Harry, and they told me they used a "special" tour guide in Egypt named Abd'El Hakim who knew the "old ways" and had profound knowledge of very ancient Egypt. I knew--then and there--that I had to meet this man.

It wasn't until over five years later—when I was ready—in November of 1992—that a series of events unfolded that enabled me to go on tour with Power Places and join a group led by Nicki Scully who had come to Egypt with the Grateful Dead in 1978 and had met Hakim and used him as guide. I discuss the amazing meeting with Hakim—guided by the Sphinx—in my first book. For the next 16 years—until his "westing" in August 2008 (almost six years to the day as I type this)—I became

Hakim's most devoted student and disciple. His teachings were truly unique, which were a result of his extraordinary background. Hakim held dual academic degrees in archaeology and Egyptology from Fouad (now Cairo) University in the early 1950s—but it was his enduring thirst for true ancient knowledge that led him to be sent by a beloved uncle as a small boy to study with Sufi masters. Hakim was an active tour guide for 56 years, having been a member of the first class of licensed guides in 1952. He had 76 years of active fieldwork, having started his career removing rubble and rocks for American Egyptologist, George Riesner, on the Giza Plateau at the tender age of six. Hakim spent his early years travelling all over Egypt to seek out and learn from the wisdom keepers who kept the great oral traditions that predated Egyptology and that have been passed down for thousands of years before there were written records. Hakim was a true Master of the Oral Tradition, and at every site he would take me to over the years, he always introduced me to the "Keepers"—old men in traditional dress who kept the "secrets."

Hakim presented to us the tradition that there had been a prehistoric, predynastic Egypt that had existed many thousands of years before the time Egyptology had labeled "ancient Egypt"—a civilization of advanced knowledge and technology that had carved the Sphinx and built the stone masonry pyramids—which were not "tombs" but machines! Hakim taught the civilization was called Khem—later known as Khemit, the "Black Land," and had existed in full glory over 10,000 years ago. Hakim had the system—I just put the label on it! Together we created the discipline of Khemitology, as opposed to Egyptology—which Hakim labeled "Greco-Roman Mythology." With his guidance, I wrote two books, *The Land of Osiris* (Adventures Unlimited Press, 2001) and *From Light into Darkness: The Evolution of Religion In Ancient Egypt* (Adventures Unlimited Press, 2005). *Land* later came out in Russian, Croatian, Italian and Czech—something both Hakim and I were proud of.

In the late 1990s Hakim and I spoke of creating a school that would continue the work and further the teachings. This dream has now become a reality; as Hakim's son Yousef and his wife, Patricia Lehman Awyan, formed the Khemit School of Ancient Mysticism in 2009. Patricia first came on tour with me in 2005 and met

Hakim and fell in love with Egypt—and Khemit. She returned in 2007, to take part in Hakim's last full tour. She returned again in 2008 and met and married Yousef. Patricia has a deep connection to the teachings and was fully embraced by Hakim and the Awyan family—as I was! I have known Yousef Abdel Hakim Awyan since he was eleven years old. He is his Father's son and so much more. The Khemit School, www.khemitology.com, has been leading tours in Egypt since 2010.

It was Hakim who is the connection between Brien Foerster and me. Neither of us remembers exactly when but it was through social media, Face book that Brien and I connected. Brien saw the video series, *The Pyramid Code*, produced by Carmen Boulter. The series featured some excellent interview clips of Hakim introducing some of the concepts of Khemitology. I had introduced Carmen to Hakim at the Cairo Airport in 1997. The series was produced in 2009. Brien relates how he was instantly drawn to Hakim, his voice, his energy, his knowledge and his wisdom. Brien soon found me on Face book—and the rest is history.

This book is the result of two trips Brien Foerster has taken to Egypt—on tour with the Khemit School in April 2013 and 2014. We called these tours "Techno-Spiritual"—as the ancient Khemitians did not differentiate between the two—and the tour in 2013 featured my dear friend and esteemed colleague, Christopher Dunn. Brien came to Egypt with not only his mind and eyes open, but with an open heart, too. Because of this, not only ancient Khemit but modern Egypt and her people opened to him. Because of the great connections of Yousef Awyan, who carries the mantle of his father, and Mohamed Ibrahim, our Tour Director and Egyptologist; Brien was able to see and experience many things "normal" researchers and tourists—even Egyptologists—have never seen! I have said Brien's first two trips were like the first five for me—we found so many new things. This book contains his wonderful insights gained through his vast knowledge of ancient South American, Polynesian and Micronesian, and many Native cultures. The photos contained in this book are fresh and current, and the understanding Brien demonstrates throughout the text is uniquely profound. "Lay people" and professionals alike will enjoy and gain from Brien Foerster's deep insights and powers of observation. I look forward to many more hours in the field with Brien—in my beloved Egypt and his beloved Peru.

Stephen S. Mehler, M.A.

The author with Stephen Mehler at JFK airport on the way to Cairo in 2013

Table Of Contents

1/ Introduction

2/ Aswan Quarry

3/ Elephantine Island

4/ Tombs of the Nobles

5/ Ramesseum

6/ Colossi of Memnon

7/ Dendera

8/ Abydos

9/ Karnak

10/ Meidum

11/ Dashur

12/ Saqqara

13/ Abusir

14/ Abugurab

15/ Giza Plateau

16/ Bibliography

1/ Introduction

Egypt, or more specifically ancient Egypt is a subject that has fascinated people from around the world since Napoleon Bonaparte, for example, arranged the first studies in Egyptology when he brought some 150 scientists and artists to study and document Egypt's natural history, which was published in the *Description de l'Égypte*. (1) That was a series of publications, appearing first in 1809 and continuing until the final volume appeared in 1829, which offered a comprehensive scientific description of ancient and modern Egypt as well as its natural history.

It was the collaborative work of about 160 civilian scholars and scientists, known popularly as the savants, who accompanied Napoleon's expedition to Egypt in 1798 to 1801 as part of the French Revolutionary Wars, as well as about 2000 artists and technicians, including 400 engravers, who would later compile it into a full work.

Engraving made from Napoleon's visit

The history of Egypt has been tumultuous; to say the least in the at least 5000 years since the rise of the first leaders, the so called pharaohs. Rather than there being a smooth succession of rulers from the first until the last, major periods of internal rivalry and foreign invasion left scars on the land. Historical records were deliberately or accidentally destroyed, such as the burning of the library of Alexandria, and many of the great temples and pyramids were damaged or destroyed by people later than their builders. In many cases the reason for the damage was to erase the existence of an earlier ruler and his accomplishments, or to build new structures from a site that was no longer considered relevant.

The Royal Library of Alexandria, or Ancient Library of Alexandria, in Alexandria, Egypt, was one of the largest and most significant libraries of the ancient world. It was dedicated to the Muses, the nine goddesses of the arts. (2) It flourished under the patronage of the Ptolemaic dynasty and functioned as a major center of scholarship from its construction in the 3rd century BC until the Roman conquest of Egypt in 30 BC. With collections of works, lecture halls, meeting rooms, and gardens, the library was part of a larger research institution called the Museum of Alexandria, where many of the most famous thinkers of the ancient world studied.

Drawing of what the library of Alexandria may have looked like

The library was created by Ptolemy I Soter, who was a Macedonian general and the successor of Alexander the Great. (3) As a symbol of the wealth and power of Egypt, it employed many scribes to steal books from around the known world, copy them, and never returned them. Most of the books were kept as papyrus scrolls, and though it is unknown how many such scrolls were housed at any given time, their combined value was incalculable. The library is famous for having been burned resulting in the loss of many scrolls and books, and has become a symbol of the destruction of cultural knowledge. A few sources differ on who is responsible for the destruction and when it occurred. Although there is a mythology of the burning of the Library at Alexandria, it may have suffered several fires or acts of destruction over many years.

Possible occasions for the partial or complete destruction of the Library of Alexandria include a fire set by Julius Caesar in 48 BC, an attack by Aurelian in the 270s AD, the decree of Coptic Pope Theophilus in 391 AD, and the decree of the second caliph Omar ibn Al-khattāb in 640 AD. After the main library was fully destroyed, ancient scholars used a "daughter library" in a temple known as the Serapeum, located in another part of the city. According to Socrates of Constantinople, Coptic Pope Theophilus destroyed the Serapeum in 391 AD.

As the library was first built, and its collections gathered under the rule of the Ptolemaic dynasty, as in the Greeks, one has to wonder if it was in fact a complete record of all of Egyptian history. The Ptolemies were quite unlike other foreigners who had ruled Egypt in several respects. Most importantly, they ruled within Egypt. One of the best phrases for understanding the nature of their government's relationship with the country on which they imposed their rule is that "the Ptolemies used Egypt." By contrast, it is fair to say that "the Romans abused Egypt." The Greeks could use Egypt because they came upon a well-developed country in respect to its economic, intellectual, and political life. These factors were in force to an extent which was unparalleled anywhere else within the Hellenistic world where the Greeks had placed themselves to rule over indigenous populations. In the case of Egypt, the Ptolemies found themselves in control of a highly sophisticated ancient civilization and administration, not a group of cloddish barbarians. The Egyptians had as high a level of culture as the Greeks, but it was quite different from theirs. (4)

The idea that the Greeks were of as high a cultural level is a dubious point when you take into account how long each civilization had existed prior to their engagement. In the 8th century BC, Greece began to emerge from the Dark Ages which followed the fall of the Mycenaean civilization. Literacy had been lost and Mycenaean script forgotten, but the Greeks adopted the Phoenician alphabet, modifying it to create the Greek alphabet. From about the 9th century BC written records began to appear. (5) Greece was divided into many small self-governing communities, a pattern largely dictated by Greek geography: every island, valley and plain is cut off from its neighbours by the sea or mountain ranges.

A mercantile class arose in the first half of the 7th century, shown by the introduction of coinage in about 680 BC. This seems to have introduced tension to many city states. The aristocratic regimes which generally governed were threatened by the new-found wealth of merchants, who in turn desired political power. Athens suffered a land and agrarian crisis in the late 7th century, again resulting in civil strife. The Archon (chief magistrate) Draco made severe reforms to the law code in 621 BC (hence "draconian"), but these failed to quell the conflict. Eventually the moderate reforms of Solon (594 BC), improving the lot of the poor but firmly entrenching the aristocracy in power, gave Athens some stability.

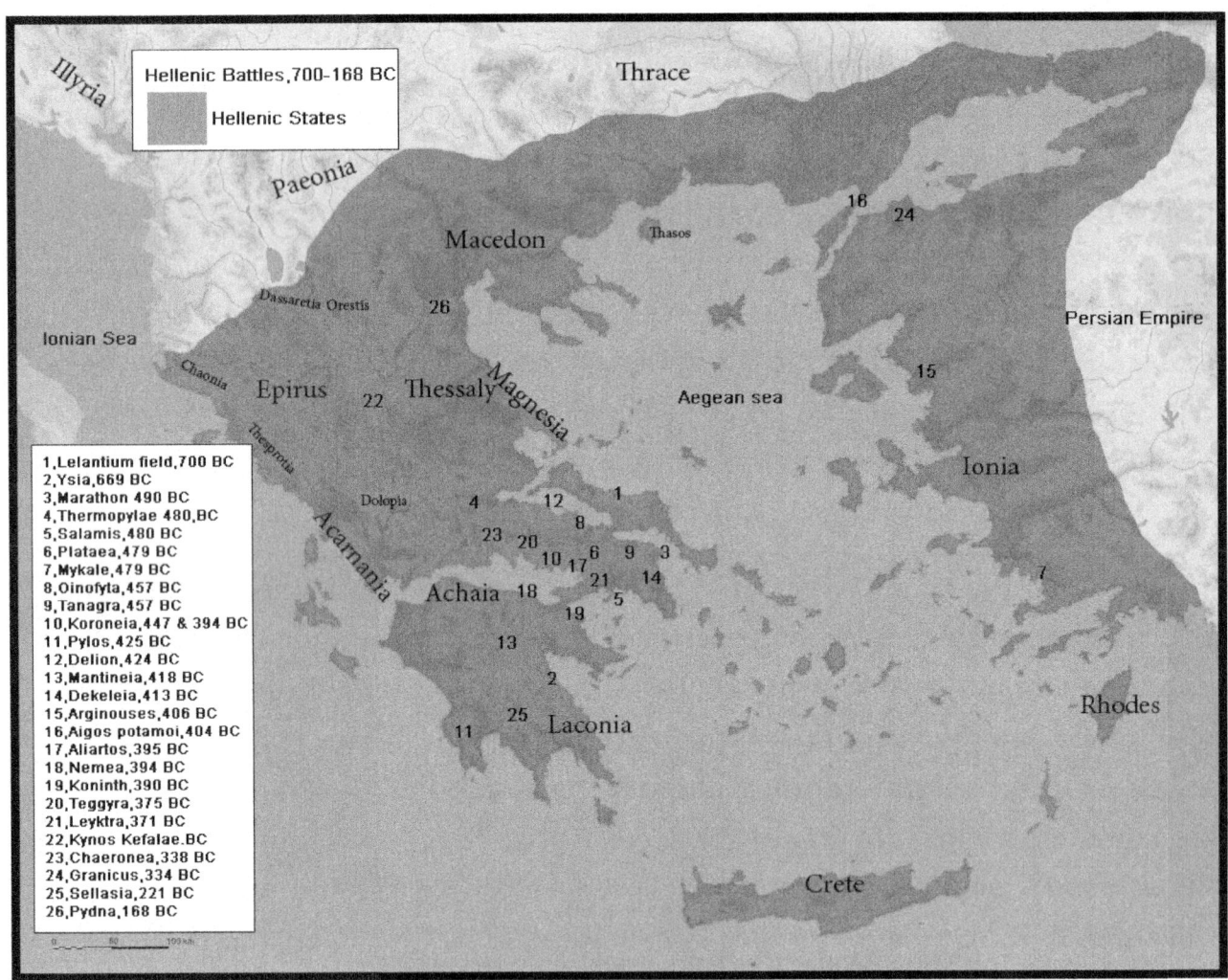

Battles occurring in classical Greek times

Two major wars shaped the Classical Greek world. The Persian Wars (500 to 448 BC) are recounted in Herodotus's *Histories*. Ionian Greek cities revolted from the Persian Empire and were supported by some of the mainland cities, eventually led by Athens. The wars had left devastation in their wake. Discontent with the Spartan hegemony that followed induced the Thebans to attack. Their general, Epaminondas, crushed Sparta at the Battle of Leuctra in 371 BC, inaugurating a period of Theban dominance in Greece. In 346 BC, unable to prevail in its ten-year war with Phocis, Thebes called upon Philip II of Macedon for aid. Macedon quickly forced the city states into being united by the League of Corinth which led to the conquering of the Persian Empire and the Hellenistic Age had begun. Soon Alexander the Great conquered Egypt at an early stage of his great journey of conquests, which lasted from 332 to 323 BC. He respected the pharaohnic religions and customs and he was declared by the priest, pharaoh of Egypt. However, according to Stephen Mehler it was more that he was appointed *High Priest of Amen,* and not pharaoh, which Stephen and the Khemit School believe to have been the title of the female, not male in the society back into deep antiquity. *Pharaoh* seems to be the Greek form of the earlier term *Per-Aah*, meaning *high house* in Khemitian.

Compare this now with the history of Egypt, which has always been centered near the life giving Nile River, center of somewhat stable agricultural production for thousands of years. A unified kingdom was founded according to most Egyptologists around 3150 BC by King Menes, leading to a series of dynasties that ruled Egypt for the next three millennia. Egyptian culture flourished during this long period and remained distinctively Egyptian in its religion, arts, language and customs. The first two ruling dynasties of a unified Egypt set the stage for the Old Kingdom period, 2700 to 2200 BC., which constructed many pyramids; most notably the Third Dynasty pyramid of Djoser at Saqqara and some believe the Fourth Dynasty Giza Pyramids.

The First Intermediate Period ushered in a time of political upheaval for about 150 years. (6) Stronger Nile floods and stabilization of government, however, brought back renewed prosperity for the country in the Middle Kingdom *c.* 2040 BC, reaching a peak during the reign of Pharaoh Amenemhat III. A second period of disunity heralded the arrival of the first foreign ruling dynasty in Egypt, that of the Semitic Hyksos. The Hyksos invaders took over much of Lower Egypt around 1650 BC and founded a new capital at Avaris. They were driven out by an Upper

Egyptian force led by Ahmose I, who founded the Eighteenth Dynasty and relocated the capital from Memphis to Thebes.

The New Kingdom, 1550 to 1070 BC, began with the Eighteenth Dynasty, marking the rise of Egypt as an international power that expanded during its greatest extension to an empire as far south as Tombos in Nubia, and included parts of the Levant in the east. This period is noted for some of the most well-known Pharaohs, including Hatshepsut, Thutmose III, Akhenaten and his wife Nefertiti, Tutankhamun and Ramesses II. The first historically attested expression of monotheism came during this period as Atenism, led by Akhenaten and Nefertiti until the Amun (or Amen) priesthood, who had previously been in power, took over once again. Frequent contacts with other nations brought new ideas to the New Kingdom. The country was later invaded and conquered by Libyans, Nubians and Assyrians, but native Egyptians eventually drove them out and regained control of their country. (7) The Thirtieth Dynasty was the last native ruling dynasty during the Pharaohnic epoch. It fell to the Persians in 343 BC after the last native Pharaoh, King Nectanebo II, was defeated in battle. Soon after, Alexander the Great entered the land.

Relief carving of Akhenaten's family

For it to be suggested that the Greeks had as high a level of culture, and with that scientific and artistic achievement, taking into account their incredibly war like tendencies which seemingly resulted in long periods of social instability as that of the Egyptians is most likely naïve. Though Egypt had its fair share of disputes, both internal and external, it was relatively stable for 3000 years. This could have led to prolonged cultural evolution, or at least retention of what was known of science and art up until the Greek, and worst yet Roman occupations.

Egyptology is the study of ancient Egyptian history, language, literature, religion, architecture and art from the 5th millennium BC until the end of its native religious practices in the 4th century AD. A practitioner of the discipline is called an "Egyptologist". In Europe, particularly continental Europe, Egyptology is primarily regarded as being a philological discipline (the study of language in written historical sources,) while in North America it is often regarded as a branch of archaeology.

Some of the first historical accounts of Egypt were given to us by Herodotus, Strabo, Diodorus Siculus and the largely lost work of Manetho, who was an Egyptian priest during the reign of Ptolemy I and Ptolemy II in the 3rd century BC. The Ptolemies were very much interested in the work of the ancient Egyptians, and many of the monuments, including the pyramids, were restored by them (although they built many new temples in the Egyptian style.) The Romans too carried out restoration work in this most ancient of lands.

Abdul Latif al-Baghdadi, a teacher at Cairo's Al-Azhar University in the 13th century, wrote detailed descriptions on ancient Egyptian monuments.(8) Similarly, the 15th-century Egyptian historian al-Maqrizi wrote detailed accounts of Egyptian antiquities. European exploration and travel writings of ancient Egypt commenced from the 13th century onward, with only occasional detours into a more scientific approach, notably by Claude Sicard, Benoît de Maillet, Frederic Louis Norden and Richard Pococke. In the early 17th century, John Greaves measured the pyramids, having inspected the broken Obelisk of Domitian in Rome, and then destined for the Earl of Arundel's collection in London. (9) He went on to publish the illustrated *Pyramidographia* in 1646, while the Jesuit scientist-priest Athanasius Kircher was perhaps the first to hint at the phonetic importance of Egyptian hieroglyphs, demonstrating Coptic as a vestige of early Egyptian, for which he is considered a "founder" of Egyptology. In the late 18th century, with Napoleon's scholars' recording of Egyptian flora, fauna and history, published as *Description de l'Egypte* the study of many aspects of ancient Egypt became more scientifically oriented. And when the British captured Egypt from the French and gained the Rosetta stone. Modern Egyptology is generally perceived as beginning about 1822.

The Rosetta stone in the British Museum in London

The Rosetta stone is a granodiorite stele inscribed with a decree issued at Memphis in 196 BCE on behalf of King Ptolemy V. The decree appears in three scripts: the upper text is ancient Egyptian hieroglyphs, the middle portion Demotic script (the stage of the Egyptian language following Late Egyptian and preceding Coptic,) and the lowest Ancient Greek. Because it presents essentially the same text in all three scripts (with some minor differences among them), it provided the key to the modern understanding of Egyptian hieroglyphs.

Study of the decree was already under way as the first full translation of the Greek text appeared in 1803. It was 20 years, however, before the transliteration of the Egyptian scripts was announced by Jean-François Champollion in Paris in 1822; it took longer still before scholars were able to read Ancient Egyptian inscriptions and literature confidently. Major advances in the decoding were recognition that the stone offered three versions of the same text (1799); that the demotic text used phonetic characters to spell foreign names (1802); that the hieroglyphic text did so as well, and had pervasive similarities to the demotic (Thomas Young, 1814); and that, in addition to being used for foreign names, phonetic characters were also used to spell native Egyptian words (Champollion, 1822 to 1824).

Though the Rosetta stone has clearly proven useful, questions arise from some Egyptian hieroglyphic experts as to its accuracy, especially the validity and depth of meaning of the ancient Egyptian glyphs. Since the Rosetta stone was the work of scribes during the time of Greek occupation, the ancient Egyptian meanings could simply be the superficial aspects, rather than the deeper expressions of the priestly class, for example. Author Laird Scranton, in his first book, *The Science of the Dogon*, demonstrated that the cosmological structure described in the myths and drawings of the Dogon (an ethnic group living in the central plateau region of the country of Mali, in Western Africa) runs parallel to modern science (atomic theory, quantum theory, and string theory), with Dogon drawings often taking the same form as accurate scientific diagrams that relate to the formation of matter.

Scranton also pointed to the close resemblance between the keywords and component elements of Dogon cosmology and those of ancient Egypt as well as to the implication that ancient cosmology may also be about actual science. *Sacred Symbols of the Dogon* uses these parallels as the starting point for a new interpretation of the Egyptian hieroglyphic language. By substituting Dogon cosmological drawings for equivalent glyph shapes in Egyptian words, a new way of reading and interpreting the Egyptian hieroglyphs emerges. Scranton shows how each hieroglyph constitutes an entire concept and that their meanings are scientific in nature. Using the Dogon symbols as a "Rosetta stone," he reveals references within the ancient Egyptian language that define the full range of scientific components of matter.

Abd'El Hakim Awyan did not feel that Champollion's translations were of any depth, since the Greeks themselves were not privy to the depths of the meanings of the symbols (from personal consultations with Stephen Mehler.)

Dogon village in a recent photo

Therefore, the exclusive use of the Rosetta stone as a way to translate Egyptian hieroglyphics and therefore interpret what they are saying may be a superficial exercise, with the deeper meanings being lost. What this means is that Egyptology may just be brushing the surface of the history of ancient Egypt, and this comes into play here especially when we look at some, and I must stress some of the ancient structures of Egypt and what they were originally made for, and by whom.

Egyptology's modern history begins with the invasion of Egypt by Napoleon Bonaparte. The subsequent publication of Description de l'Egypte between 1809 and 1829 made numerous ancient Egyptian source materials available to Europeans for the first time. Jean François Champollion, Thomas Young and Ippolito Rosellini were some of the first Egyptologists of wide acclaim. The German Karl Richard Lepsius was an early participant in the investigations of Egypt; mapping, excavating, and recording several sites. Champollion announced his general decipherment of the system of Egyptian hieroglyphics for the first time, employing the Rosetta stone as his primary aid. With subsequently ever increasing knowledge of Egyptian writing and language, the study of ancient Egyptian civilization was able to proceed with greater academic rigour and with all the added impetus that comprehension of the written sources was able to engender. Egyptology became more professional via work of William Matthew Flinders Petrie, among others. Petrie introduced techniques of field preservation, recording, and excavating. Howard Carter's expedition and discovery of Tutankhamun brought much acclaim to the field of Egyptology. Many highly educated amateurs now also travelled to Egypt, however, including women such as Harriet Martineau and Florence Nightingale, who both left fascinatingly philosophical accounts of their travels, which revealed learned familiarity with all the latest European Egyptology.

William Flinders Petrie as a young man in Egypt

It must be stressed that we owe a tremendous debt of gratitude to all of the Egyptologists for they have provided us with invaluable information about the lives and achievements of the dynastic Egyptians from 3100 BC onwards. What this book will address are those constructions for which Egyptology, in my estimation does not have satisfactory answers as to who made them, when and why. The approach to this will be similar to my Legacy; Vintage Photos Of Ancient Egypt. We will explore from the most southern part of Egypt, so called Upper Egypt and move northwards, into what was known as Lower Egypt, discussing some of the puzzling works that are not properly explained along the way.

2/ Aswan Quarry

Aswan is the ancient city of Swenet, which in antiquity was the frontier town of ancient Egypt facing the south. Swenet is supposed to have derived its name from an Egyptian goddess with the same name. This goddess later was identified as Eileithyia by the Greeks and Lucina by the Romans during their occupation of ancient Egypt because of the similar association of their goddesses with childbirth, and of which means "the opener". The ancient name of the city also is said to be derived from the Egyptian symbol for trade, (10) and the Khemit School contend that it meant "The Beginning of the Waters" in ancient Khemitian, named after a much older city in the south where the Nile entered the land of Khemit, *The Black Land.*

Because the ancient Egyptians oriented toward the origin of the life giving waters of the Nile in the south, Swenet was the first town in the country, and Egypt always was conceived to "open" or begin at Swenet. The city stood upon a peninsula on the right (east) bank of the Nile, immediately below (and north of) the first cataract of the flowing waters, which extend to it from Philae. Navigation to the delta was possible from this location without encountering a barrier. The stone quarries of ancient Egypt located here were celebrated for their stone, and especially for the granitic rock called Syenite, which is usually pink or red in appearance. They furnished the colossal statues, obelisks, and monolithic shrines that are found throughout Egypt, including the pyramids; and the traces of the quarrymen who wrought in these 3,000 years ago are still visible in the native rock.

Astonishing flat wall at the Aswan quarry

Today there are 2 unfinished obelisks, one large and another much smaller that still lie in the quarry, attached firmly to the bedrock. Archaeologists claim the pharaoh known as Hatshepsut sanctioned the construction of the bigger of the two. It is nearly one third larger than any ancient Egyptian obelisk ever erected. If finished it would have measured around 42 m (approximately 137 feet) and would have weighed nearly 1,200 tons. (11) Archeologists speculate that it was intended to complement the so-called Lateran Obelisk which was originally at Karnak and is now outside the Lateran Palace in Rome. The obelisk's creators began to carve it directly out of bedrock, but cracks appeared in the granite and the project was abandoned. Originally it was thought that the stone had an undetected flaw (see photo) and thus work stopped abruptly on it.

Trench at the unfinished obelisk showing crack

The greatest questions that arise are, what tools could have been used to shape this massive stone monument, and how were the Egyptians planning on raising it out of the pit in which it sits, taking into account its immense size. To the former, most Egyptologists believe that round and hand held stone dolerite pounders were the main tools being used. Dolerite is a volcanic rock. While similar to basalt, it contains crystals which can be seen with a hand lens. This indicates that it cooled a little more slowly than basalt. Typically it is found in volcanic plugs which channelled the basalt to the surface. Dolerite contains pyroxene which is a hard silicate mineral with a hardness of 5 to 6.5 on what is called the Mohs scale.

Conventional pockets made for insertion of wooden wedges

The Mohs scale of mineral hardness characterizes the scratch resistance of various minerals through the ability of a harder material to scratch a softer material. It was created in 1812 by the German geologist and mineralogist Friedrich Mohs and is one of several definitions of hardness in materials science. As the hardest known naturally occurring substance when the scale was designed, diamonds are at the top of the scale and have the maximum value of 10, while all other materials have a lesser value.

Dolorite pounders at the quarry at Aswan

In basic terms, any tool should have a greater hardness than the material being cut or shaped. The pink granite of which the unfinished obelisk is composed has a Mohs hardness that sits between the scale of 6 and 7, and thus is more or less the same hardness as dolerite, making the latter a poor material for shaping the former. Also, Aswan granite contains between 45 and 55% quartz crystal, which has a Mohs value of 7, thus making this granite especially difficult to work with Bronze, the other tool substance known to and used by the ancient Egyptians is much softer, being on average 3.5 on the Mohs scale. If dolerite pounders were used to shape the granite, the tools would basically wear out as fast as the material being worked on, and sounds like an unlikely candidate.

I myself tried to make an impression in a granite surface at the Aswan quarry using one of the many dolerite pounders that lay around the site. After 15 repeated hard blows, not more than a few small flecks of granite were removed, and my hand hurt as a result. In order to make any real impression in the granite material, a lot of force would need to be used. The problems encountered at the unfinished obelisk is that there is very little room inside the trench to be able to create a hard blow, and such repeated efforts could also break the dolerite tool.

View of the unfinished obelisk at its base

So if stone tools were not those that were used to attempt to shape and eventually release the obelisk from its bedrock enclosure? One of the best resources for looking at alternatives is engineer and master machinist Christopher Dunn's book *Lost Technologies of Ancient Egypt: Advanced Engineering in the Temples of the Pharaohs*. As regards the unfinished obelisk at Aswan, he quotes from Nova producer Peter Tyson who tried his hand at quarrying with a dolerite pounder:

'Cupping a greenish-black dolerite ball in my hands, I brought it down with a crack onto a block of granite. Over and over, I bounced it on the same spot, till I thought I'd scrape the skin off my palms. After ten minutes, my wrists hurt from trying to guide the 12 pound rock in at an angle- the better to break the granite – and stabs of pain began shooting up my arms. Mark Lehner (a major proponent of the dolerite pounder theory) recalled that after once pounding for several hours, he could barely type on a computer. I did it for only 20 minutes, and all I had to show for it was a baby's palmful of granite dust. And the granite's surface looked no different than when I'd stated.'

According to Dunn himself:

'The unfinished obelisk offers compelling indirect evidence regarding the level of technology its creator's had reached – not so much by indicating clearly what methods were used, but by the overpowering indications of what methods could not have been used.'

Chris Dunn's opinion is that if one obvious the pattern left by the tool which did the actual shaping, especially in the walls of the trenches that surround the unfinished obelisk, there is an even pattern which would unlikely have occurred if hand tools such as the pounders were used. According to Chris:

'The horizontal striations are typical in cutting when the feed of a tool that is removing material pauses along its path, withdrawn to remove waste, and the interruption of the tool leaves a mark on the surface. Also, it could be that as the tool was rocked back and forth against the walls of the trench to clear the waste on the vertical wall, horizontal striations appeared where the tool pressed the cutting surface against the side wall to keep the trench from narrowing.'

He believes that the obelisk channel was cut using a tool that functioned similar to a chain saw, except it was much wider as the intention was to remove as much material as possible in an efficient manner. In essence he is describing something akin to a giant belt sander apparatus attached to a huge guided machine. In his own words:

'To suggest, however, that the ancient Egyptians used megamachines in prehistory is stretching the evidence to limits that are unacceptable to historians and Egyptologists. There have been no megamachines from the ancient past found in Egypt. Similarly, there have been no megamachines from prehistory found in Rome or Greece, though writings about them exist and theories about what they might have looked like have been tested.'

Scoop marks present at a smaller Aswan unfinished obelisk

My own idea is that the ancient Egyptians, and we are talking about people who lived prior to dynastic times had technology that is theoretical to us today. I am postulating that they may have had forms of energy technology which were capable of destabilizing the stone in some way. For example, if an energetic wave was emitted from a machine, and was set say to the vibrational frequency or a higher one than that of quartz crystal, it could cause that material to break. In the case of the granite from Aswan, it has very high quartz crystal content. Should this device have the capability to destabilize and break the quartz, then the surrounding materials such as mica and feldspar would simply fall away.

If this theoretical device had a focused band of energy of say 2 feet, which the center having the highest energy, then it would destabilize the stone in an arc like pattern. That pattern is what I see when I look at the quarry at Aswan.

Another view of the Aswan quarry scoop marks

As Chris Dunn stated, no large machines or anything that we would call high technology exists in the archaeological record, unless such devices in fact have been found and are hidden away in the warehouses of the Cairo museum. This statement is not made lightly. We do know that strange devices and materials have been found in archeological sites in different parts of the world, and have been labelled, boxed and hidden out of view because they do not fit the conventional historical paradigm.

Examples that can be seen in the Cairo, British and other museums are hard stone bowls and other vessels which are so amazingly round that clearly they had to have been created on lathes. A lathe is a natural development from the potter's wheel, the latter having been depicted in ancient artwork, and thus presumed to have existed in ancient Egypt. Again, the words of Chris Dunn:

'From the early origins of potter's wheels, improvements evolved the technology to what we see today, and the spinoff of the potter's wheels that are still in use are found in every manufacturing plant in the world. They have progressed from manually driven machines to water driven and steam engine driven line shaft pulleys and belts to the electric motor.'

Sir William Flinders Petrie was one of the great Egyptologists of the late 19th and early 20th centuries. In his *The Pyramids and Temples of Giza* Petrie he discusses 2 stone potsherds called 14 and 15 which he found very curious. The following is paraphrased from Chris Dunn's *Lost Technologies of Ancient Egypt* book, and are the words of Petrie himself:

'The principle of rotating the tool was, for smaller objects, abandoned in favor of rotating the work; and the lathe appears to have been as familiar an instrument in the fourth dynasty, as it is in modern workshops. The diorite (a very hard stone of about 7 on the Mohs scale) *bowls and vases of the Old Kingdom are frequently met with, and show great technical skill. One piece found at Gizeh, No.14, shows that the method employed was true turning, and not any process of grinding, since the bowl has been knocked off its centering, recentered imperfectly, and the old turning not quite turned out; thus there are two surfaces belonging to different centerings, and meeting in a cusp. Such an appearance could not be produced by any grinding or rubbing process which pressed on the surface. Another detail is shown by fragment No.15; here the curves of the bowl are spherical, and must have therefore been cut by a tool sweeping an arc from a fixed center while the bowl was rotated. That this was certainly not a chance result of hand-work is shown, not only by exact circularity of the curves, and their equality, but also by the cusp left where they meet. This has not been at all rounded off, as would certainly be the case in hand-work, and it is clear proof of the rigid mechanical method of striking curves.'*

Basalt cup or bowl in the Petrie Museum in London

Petrie also found a number of core drills, many of which are now housed in the museum named after him at the University College London in London England. The actual hollow drill bits have not been found, but the cores made of limestone, alabaster, granite and other stones have. In the words of Petrie:

'These tubular drills vary from 1/4 inch to 5 inches diameter and from 1/30 to 1/5 inch thick. The smallest hole yet found in granite is 2 inches diameter, all the lesser holes being in limestone or alabaster, which was probably worked merely with tube and sand. A peculiar feature of these cores is that they are always tapered, and the holes are always enlarged towards the top. In the soft stones cut merely with loose powder, such a result would naturally be produced simply by the dead weight on the drill head, which forced it into the stone, not being truly balanced, and so always pulling the drill over to one side ; as it rotated this would grind off material from both the core and the hole. But in the granite core, No.7, such an

explanation is insufficient, since the deep cutting grooves are scored out quite as strongly in the tapered end as elsewhere; and if the taper was merely produced by rubbing of powder, they would have been polished away, and certainly could not be equally deep in quartz as in feldspar. Hence we are driven to the conclusion that auxiliary cutting points were inserted along the side, as well as around the edge of the tube drill; as no granite or diorite cores are known under two inches diameter, there would be no impossibility in setting such stones, working either through a hole in the opposite side of the drill, or by setting a stone in a hole cut through the drill, and leaving it to project both inside and outside the tube. Then a preponderance of the top weight to any side would tilt the drill so as to wear down the groove wider and wider, and thus enable the drill and the dust to be the more easily withdrawn from the groove.'

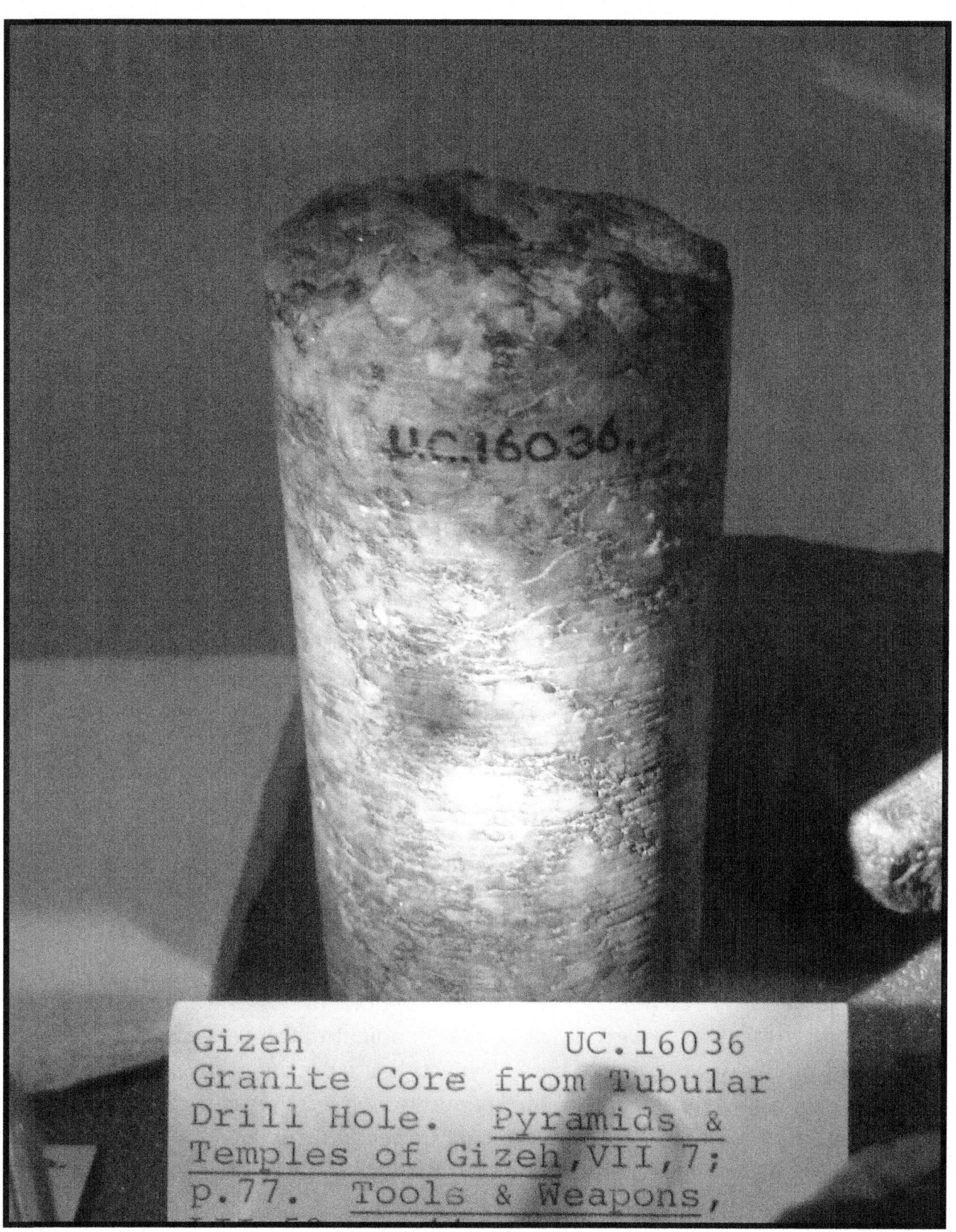

Granite drill core in the Petrie Museum

Chris Dunn spent hours in the Petrie museum and was allowed to personally examine some of the drill cores. Here he discusses the characteristics of one of them:

'The most fascinating feature of the granite core Petrie describes is the spiral groove around the core indicating a feed rate of 0.100 inch per revolution of the drill. In my article, I stated that this feed rate was 500 times faster than modern diamond drills, which penetrate at only 0.0002 inch per revolution. This has been incorrectly interpreted by some, who have concluded that a hole of the same dimension could be drilled 500 times faster by the ancient Egyptians than by modern drills. The correct way to describe the feed rate would be to say it was 500 times greater than modern diamond drills, but the rotation of the drill would not have been as fast as the modern drill's 900 revolutions per minute.'

Another amazing artifact which is on display in the Cairo museum is commonly simply called *the schist disk.* In the first wing of the Egyptian Museum of the Cairo between two rooms close to the mummy room, one cannot help but be surprised to see in a small display cabinet, although not without some difficulty caused by the reflections of the light on the crystal that covers it, a solitary object similar to a wheel or stone disc. This strange object has disturbed and continues perplexing all the Egyptologists that have had occasion to study it at great length. The first of them was its discoverer, Brian Walter Emery, one of the most important Egyptologists of 20th Century and the author of a classic volume on Egyptology, *Archaic Egypt*, which continues to be, after many years, an important bibliographical reference for the study and an understanding of the origins of the Egyptian civilization. (14)

Making excavations in 1936, in the archaeological zone of Saqqara, he discovered the Tomb of Prince Sabu, who was the son of Pharaoh Adjuib, governor of the I Dynasty (3,000 BC.) Between utensils of funeral objects that were extracted, Emery's attention was powerfully drawn to an object that he initially defined in his report on the Great Tombs of the I Dynasty as: *'a container in the form of schist bowl.'* Years later, in his previously mentioned work, Archaic Egypt, he commented on the object with a word that perfectly summarizes the reality of the situation and the discomfort the object causes; "*cachibache*" (a small hole that threatens to become a much larger hole.)

The schist disk on display in the Cairo Museum

This object is approximately 61 centimetres in diameter, and 10.6 centimetres in height in the center. It is made of schist, a very fragile and delicate rock, which requires very laborious carving. Its form resembles that of a plate or a concave steering wheel of a car, with a series of three cuts or curved "shovels" that resemble the helix of a boat, and in the center, an orifice with a rim that acts as the outside receiver of some axis of a wheel or some other unknown mechanism, arranged to turn. As is well known, the official position maintained by Egyptology with respect to the appearance and use of the wheel on the part of the Egyptians is very clear and leaves no room for doubt. The introduction of the wheel in Egypt they assure us coincided with the invasion of the Hyksos at the end of the Medium Empire, in 1640 BC. They used it, on among other things, their military chariots. However, the potter's wheel may have predated this.

The question then is inevitable: if it is not a wheel, what is the strange object that appeared in the Tomb of Prince Sabu, 1,400 years before the invasion of the Hyksos? In spite of the complexity of this problem, the subject has become even more serious as a result of the technical studies that a variety of investigators have made, impelled by the surprising and strange design of this device. As well, the Egyptologist Cyril Aldred reached the conclusion that, independently of what the object was used for or what it represented, its design was without a doubt, a copy of a previous, much older metallic object. In fact, this schist wheel appeared in Tomb of Prince Sabu along with other strange copper objects, which along with some bronze, gold and silver was practically the only metal that the Egyptians then had.

The doubt that has been plaguing us is wondering how the ancient Egyptians could design so delicate and complex a structural object more than 5,000 years ago. A structure that in the case of the three strange cuts or curved shovels, induces one to think almost immediately about its use in relation to moving air or water. It also makes us suspect that this object is only a small part of a more complex mechanism, and that it was saved thanks to a stone reproduction for some unknown reason, made by an artist, with unknown tools. According to the typical and expected view of the archaeologists and Egyptologists, this object is no more than a tray or the pedestal of some candelabrum, with a design a product of blind chance.

I am personally quite amazed that such a controversial piece is still on display in the Cairo museum, and wonder what even odder objects are hidden away in their warehouses.

3/ Elephantine Island

Known to the Ancient Egyptians as Abu or Yebu, and Bu Ab according to the Khemit School, meaning "Land of the Large Animal" the island of Elephantine stood at the border between Egypt and Nubia. It was an excellent defensive site for a city and its location made it a natural cargo transfer point for river trade. This border is near the Tropic of Cancer, the most northerly latitude at which the sun can appear directly overhead at noon and from which it appears to reverse direction or "turn back" at the solstices. According to Egyptian mythology, here was the dwelling place of Khnum, the ram-headed god of the cataracts, who guarded and controlled the waters of the Nile from caves beneath the island. He was worshipped here as part of a late triad among the Egyptian pantheon of deities.

There are records of an Egyptian temple to Khnum on the island as early as the third Dynasty of Egypt. This temple was completely rebuilt in the Late Period, during the thirtieth dynasty of Egypt, just before the foreign rule that followed in the Greco-Roman Period. The Greeks formed the Ptolemaic dynasty during their three hundred year rule over Egypt (305 to 30 BC) and maintained the ancient religious customs and traditions, while often associating the Egyptian deities with their own. Then Egypt was ruled by the Roman and Byzantine Empires, and its religious traditions existed alongside those from diverse cultures, until Islamic rule began circa 600 AD.

Water worn granite near Elephantine Island

Many of the sites have been badly damaged over the course of thousands of years, and from a *lost ancient technology* standpoint the most interesting artifacts are found on the north side, in an area which was where older stone works were recycled by later ages or cultures. Foremost among the artifacts are two recessed blocks of astonishing precision. One, thankfully for us is almost intact, and lies on its back, while the other has been broken into several pieces. When they were originally created is unknown, but the quality of the workmanship is far superior to presumably more recent works of known age.

They are made of Aswan granite, which as discussed earlier would be a challenge, to say the least for the bronze tools of the dynastic Egyptians. Around 3000 BC, iron was a scarce and precious metal in the Near East. The earliest known iron artifacts are nine small beads, dated to 3200 BC, from burials in Gerzeh, northern Egypt, that were made from meteoric iron, and shaped by careful hammering. (15) Iron's qualities, in contrast to those of bronze, were not understood. Between 1200 BC and 1000 BC, diffusion in the understanding of iron metallurgy and use of iron objects was fast and far-flung. In the history of ferrous metallurgy, iron smelting, the extraction of usable metal from oxidized iron ores is more difficult than tin and copper smelting. These other metals and their alloys can be worked cold, or melted in simple pottery kilns and cast in molds; but smelted iron requires hot working and can be melted only in specially designed furnaces. It is therefore not surprising that humans only mastered iron smelting after several millennia of bronze metallurgy.

Stephen Mehler and Yousef Awyan of the Khemit School at Elephantine Island

In the Black Pyramid of Abusir, dating before 2000 BC, Gaston Maspero found some pieces of iron. In the funeral text of Pepi I, the metal is mentioned. Iron metal is singularly scarce in collections of Egyptian antiquities. Bronze remained the primary material there until the conquest by Assyria between 673 and 663 BC. The explanation of this would seem to lie in the fact that the relics are in most cases the paraphernalia of tombs, the funeral vessels and vases, and iron being considered an impure metal by the ancient Egyptians it was never used in their manufacture of these or for any religious purposes.

Anthony, Tony and the author inspecting a rose granite artifact

The Greeks and Romans, who occupied Egypt of course had iron tools at their disposal, but did not tend to work in hard stone like granite, preferring the much softer limestone and alabaster, as well as marble to some extent. So if the dynastic Egyptians, Greeks and Romans did not make these two massive precise objects, as well as many others that we shall explore, then who did? This is where we introduce the concept of the Khemitians, who were people that lived long before the three previously mentioned groups, and seemingly had lost ancient high technology.

Most Egyptologists and lay people know that Egypt is derived from the Greek word *Aegyptos*. But few have ever traced the origin of the word. According to author Stephen Mehler in his first book *Land Of Osiris: An Introduction To Khemitology, Aegyptos* is a contraction of the Greek term *Hi-Gi-Ptos*. *Hi-Gi-Ptos* was a Greek transliteration of the ancient term *Het-Ka-Ptah*. *Het (Hit, Hat)* meant "place," and *Ka* is a term that has been subjected to many translations by Egyptologists.

Khat or *Khet* is the personality that attaches itself to the body, while *Ptah* was the title of one of the so-called "Creator Gods" or Neters. So the term *Het-Ka-Ptah* meant the "Place of the Projection of the Principle of Ptah" or the "Place where the Projection of Ptah Manifested." This term is found as an inscription on a stela near the modern Egyptian village of Mit Rahaina situated near the ruins of the ancient Egyptian capital city the Greeks named Memphis, known to the ancients as *Men-Nefer* (The Generation of Harmony). Therefore, the term *Het-Ka-Ptah* referred only to one site, one city that was the first capital of Dynastic Egypt, not the whole country or civilization. The ancients referred to their land as *KMT*, which has been written many different ways: *Kemet, Kemit, Khemet, Khem, and Al Khem*. As stated earlier, it literally meant "the Black Land" and referred to the rich, black alluvial soil deposited by the Nile River, which allowed the agricultural basis of the civilization to flourish. The indigenous tradition of Egypt tells us the civilization was Khemit, and the people and language were called *Khemitian*. (16)

Khemit School tour member and a black granite artifact partially quarried

It is from Khemit that we get the words alchemy as well chemistry, and from the word *Neter* that the Greeks derived our present word nature. In 1992, Stephen met Egyptian born Egyptologist and Indigenous Wisdom Keeper, Abd'El Hakim Awyan. It is Hakim's teachings about the ancient Khemitian civilization, well over 10,000 years old that forms the basis of Stephen's work, as well as that of the Awyan descendants who operate the Khemit School at Giza. Born and raised in the small village of Nazlet El Saman at the very edge of the Giza Plateau, with its Pyramids and Sphinx, Abd'El Hakim Awyan developed an interest in the true origins of the many monuments and artifacts of ancient Egypt from a very young age. His keen insight guided him to see a totally different view of Egypt's past than what has been written by traditional historians. Hakim, whose name means "the wise one" or "wise healer", quickly felt a deep connection to the information as he learned and discovered it. Driven by a need to know more, he embarked on a lifelong study of the full scope, and possible impact that this information might have on our world. He utilized the knowledge gained from acquiring degrees in both archaeology and Egyptology throughout his 50 years of fieldwork, travelling throughout Egypt, researching and studying at the many sacred sites.

Combining his education, field experience, and inner guidance, Hakim was able to reveal that the ancient Egyptians, or Khemitians, as he called them, were far more technologically and spiritually advanced than history has given them credit for. In recent years, geologists, engineers and other experts have been able to scientifically add to the vast knowledge that Hakim collected through learning of the oral traditions of the Khemitian people and his decades of field work.

4/ Tombs of the Nobles

Cut into the high cliffs across the river from the modern city of Aswan is Qubbet el-Hawa, the site of the elite cemetery associated with the ancient town. The earliest tombs here belong to high officials of the Old Kingdom. Although the interiors are sparsely decorated, autobiographies carved into their facades provide fascinating details of the lives of these men, several of whom led trading and military expeditions south into Nubia. Other tombs here belong to nomarchs (provincial governors) from the Middle Kingdom, and New Kingdom officials.

The area is basically a massive outcrop of sandstone, with multiple bands of metallic ore deposits. Sandstone is a sedimentary rock group which is mostly made up of tiny grains of quartz. Most sandstone is formed in oceans, lakes and rivers where tiny bits of rock and dirt settle to the bottom. Year after year, these layers of sand get buried under tons of more sand and dirt until it is turned into solid rock. On the Mohs scale it averages a harness of 6.5 to 7, and thus, again, cannot be efficiently shaped with bronze tools. Some of the inner chambers and hallways are at least a few hundred feet long, and are so narrow that in places only two people can stand side by side. This would mean that if the work of removing the stone material was done by human physical work, only two individuals could be engaged in the task.

Approach to the Tombs of the Nobles across the Nile

The author and the easiest way up the trail

Khemit School group entering sandstone bedrock chambers

Yousef and Stephen decoding glyphs inside the chambers

5/ Ramesseum

The Ramesseum is the memorial temple of Pharaoh Ramesses II ("Ramesses the Great", also spelled "Ramses" and "Rameses"). It is located in the Theban necropolis in Upper Egypt, across the River Nile from the modern city of Luxor. The name – or at least its French form, Rhamesséion, was coined by Jean-François Champollion, who visited the ruins of the site in 1829 and first identified the hieroglyphs making up Ramesses's names and titles on the walls. It was originally called the *House of millions of years of Usermaatra-setepenra that unites with Thebes-the-city in the domain of Amon.* (17)

Ramesses II modified, usurped, or constructed many buildings from the ground up, and the most splendid of these, in accordance with New Kingdom Royal burial practices, would have been his memorial temple: a place of worship dedicated to pharaoh, god on earth, where his memory would have been kept alive after his death. Surviving records indicate that work on the project began shortly after the start of his reign and continued for 20 years. What is of particular interest to us here is a massive rose granite sculpture supposedly of Ramesses himself. Only fragments of the base and torso remain of the syenite statue of the enthroned pharaoh, 62 feet (19 metres) high and weighing more than 1000 tons if you include the base. (18) This was alleged to have been transported 170 miles over land. This is the largest remaining colossal statue (except statues done in situ) in the world.

The author and Yousef inspecting a giant rose granite knee

1000 tons and moved from the quarry of Aswan 170 miles away. This would be a great challenge if it was attempted today, so how could it have been done in Egyptian times? Since we know that the dynastic Egyptians had at best bronze tools, and perhaps some meteor iron implements, how could they have cut one granite block of greater than 1000 tons from the Aswan quarry, shaped it to an astonishingly precise sculpture, and then moved it 170 miles?

The author's foot versus the giant's foot

The author under the armpit of the giant

6/ Colossi of Memnon

The Colossi of Memnon (known to locals as *el-Colossat,* or *es-Salamat)* are two massive stone statues of Pharaoh Amenhotep III. For the past 3400 years (since 1350 BC) they have stood in the Theban necropolis, across the River Nile from the modern city of Luxor. At least that is the conventional Egyptologists' theory. The twin statues depict Amenhotep III (14th century BC) in a seated position, his hands resting on his knees and his gaze facing eastwards (actually SSE in modern bearings) towards the river. Two shorter figures are carved into the front throne alongside his legs: these are his wife Tiy and mother Mutemwiya. The side panels depict the Nile god Hapy.

The idea that they were created for Amenhotep III is of course based on hieroglyphic inscriptions on the thrones one which the sculptures rest. It is quite possible, as we shall see later at Karnak and other sites, that the inscribed dedication may have indeed been made during Amenhotep III's reign, but that the sculptures themselves are far older, and presumably the work of the Khemitians. The statues are made from blocks of quartzite sandstone which was quarried at el-Gabal el-Ahmar (near modern-day Cairo) and transported 675 km (420 mi) overland to Thebes. The blocks used by later Roman engineers to reconstruct the eastern colossus may have come from Edfu (north of Aswan). Including the stone platforms on which they stand which are themselves about 4 m (13 ft), the colossi reach a towering 18 m (60 ft) in height and weight of an estimated 720 tons each. (19)

The mesmerizing Colossi of Memnon

Quartzite is a hard, non-foliated metamorphic rock which was originally pure quartz sandstone. Sandstone is converted into quartzite through heating and pressure usually related to tectonic compression, and has a Mohs scale hardness of at least 7. Therefore, the Colossi of Memnon are two more candidates of what we can call examples of lost ancient high technology, and not the work of the dynastic Egyptians. Both statues are quite damaged, with the features above the waist virtually unrecognizable. The southern statue is a single piece of stone, but the eastern northern figure has a large extensive crack in the lower half and above the waist consists of 5 tiers of stone. These upper levels consist of a different type of sandstone, and are the result of a later (Roman Empire) reconstruction attempt. It is believed that originally the two statues were identical to each other, although inscriptions and minor art may have varied.

A sense of scale

In its day, this temple complex was the largest and most opulent in Egypt. Covering a total of 35 hectares (86 acres), even later rivals such as Ramesses II's Ramesseum or Ramesses III's Medinet Habu were unable to match it in area; even the Temple of Karnak, as it stood in Amenhotep's time, was smaller. With the exception of the Colossi, however, very little remains today of Amenhotep's temple. Standing on the edge of the Nile floodplain, successive annual inundations gnawed away at the foundations and it was not unknown for later rulers to dismantle, purloin, and reuse portions of their predecessors' monuments. And the Colossi, as well as the huge sculpture of the Ramesseum may indeed be much older creations, found in the same general area, and reused by Amenhotep III and Ramesses II.

7/ Dendera

The "Dendera light" is a term used to describe a supposed ancient Egyptian electrical lighting technology depicted on three stone reliefs (one single and a double representation) in the Hathor temple at the Dendera Temple complex. The sculpture became notable among some researchers because of the resemblance of the motifs to some modern electrical lighting systems. The view of Egyptologists is that the relief is a mythological depiction of a djed pillar and a lotus flower, spawning a snake within, representing aspects of Egyptian mythology. The Djed pillar is a symbol of stability which is also interpreted as the backbone of the god Osiris. In the carvings the four horizontal lines forming the capital of the djed are supplemented by human arms stretching out, as if the djed were a backbone. The arms hold up the snake within the lotus flower. The snakes coming from the lotus symbolize fertility, linked to the annual Nile flood. (20)

View of the Dendera relief carving

In contrast to the mainstream interpretation, there is a hypothesis according to which the reliefs depict ancient Egyptian electrical technology, based on comparison to similar modern devices (such as Geissler tubes, Crookes tubes, and arc lamps). (21) Some have also made the suggestion that electric lamps would explain the absence of lampblack deposits in the tombs has sometimes been forwarded as an argument supporting this particular interpretation (another argument being made is the use of a system of reflective mirrors). Proponents of this interpretation have also used a text referring to "high poles covered with copper plates" to argue this but Dr. Bolko Stern has written in detail explaining why the copper covered tops of poles do not relate to electricity or lightning, pointing out that no evidence of anything used to manipulate electricity had been found in Egypt and that this was a magical and not a technical installation. (22) However, we will discuss the idea of electricity and energy later on in this book, especially relating to the idea of wireless transmission.

An apparent giant holding up a "light bulb"

What is also intriguing about the plaques displaying the so called light bulbs is that they are located in an underground room that is very difficult to access, and thus one can presume that this chamber was meant only for initiates. As well, the plaques are made of very fine grained limestone, and were inserted into a sandstone wall, thus, they were likely brought from another, and perhaps older building.

Limestone below and sandstone above

We also find in areas outside of the main temple the presence of what are commonly known as *"key stone cuts"* which are depressions in the ends of stone blocks, more or less in the shape of a bow tie. They were theoretically created in order to either pour or implant a metal join so as to keep the stones from moving due to earthquakes or perhaps the settling of the ground underneath. Quite abundant at many of the ancient sites in Egypt, they are also found in around Cusco in Peru, Puma Punku in Bolivia, Turkey, Ankor Wat and other places where one finds very old structures.

Just of many examples of "key stone cuts"

8/ Abydos

Considered one of the most important archaeological sites in Egypt, the sacred city of Abydos was the site of many ancient temples, including Umm el-Qa'ab, a royal necropolis where early pharaohs were entombed. These tombs began to be seen as extremely significant burials and in later times it became desirable to be buried in the area, leading to the growth of the town's importance as a cultural site. Today, Abydos is notable for the memorial temple of Seti I, which contains an inscription from the nineteenth dynasty known to the modern world as the Abydos King List. It is a chronological list showing cartouches of most dynastic pharaohs of Egypt from Menes until Ramesses I, Seti's father. The Great Temple and most of the ancient town are buried under the modern buildings to the north of the Seti temple.

Khemit School at the Great Temple

What are of particular interest to us here are hieroglyphics which some believe represent modern machines, and the surreal Osirion. The *Helicopter hieroglyphs* refer to a cartouche carving from the Temple of Seti I. In paleocontact hypothesis circles (ancient aliens or ancient astronauts) the hieroglyphics have been interpreted as an out of place artifact depicting a helicopter as well as other examples of modern technology, such as an army tank and submarine or air plane. This claim is dismissed by Egyptologists who highlight this pareidolia (a psychological phenomenon involving a vague and random stimulus, often an image or sound being perceived as significant) is partly based on widely distributed retouched images that removed key details from the actual carvings. The anomaly is the creation of a cartouche being reused by following generations, and is referred to as *palimpset* according to Stephen Mehler. The initial carving was made during the reign of Seti I, and the stone was later reused during the period of Ramesses II with one carving being on top of the other. (23)

Proposed machines on one wall

The Osirion or Osirion is located at the rear of the temple of Seti I. It is an integral part of Seti I's funeral complex and is built to resemble an 18th dynasty Valley of the Kings tomb. It was discovered by archaeologists Flinders Petrie and Margaret Murray who were excavating the site in 1902 to 1903. The Osirion was originally built at a considerably lower level than the foundations of the temple of Seti, who ruled from 1294 to 1279 BC. (24) While there is disagreement as to its true age, despite the fact that it is situated at a lower depth than the structures nearby, that it features a very different architectural approach, and that it is frequently flooded with water which would have made carving it impossible had the water level been the same at the time of construction, Peter Brand says it "can be dated confidently to Seti's reign." (25)

Looking into the megalithic Osirion

And how does Mr. Brand come to that conclusion? The construction of the Osirion is nothing like that of other buildings in the Abydos complex. As was stated earlier, all of the Osirion is below the level of the other buildings, and is composed of Aswan granite and quartzite, whereas the others are predominantly limestone. The vertical granite columns in the Osirion show a remarkable level of precision, which again would most likely be beyond the capability of dynastic builders, and some estimates are that each column weighs up to 60 tons.

Osirion in an uncharacteristically dry state

The basic design, execution and materials used are far more similar to the Valley Temple and Sphinx Temple on the Giza Plateau than the other buildings at Abydos, and thus clearly stand out, as it is the only massive granite construction known of in southern Egypt. Another feature of the Osirion which has caused great controversy is the *flower of life* symbols found on some of the columns. A *flower of life* figure consists of seven or more overlapping circles, in which the center of each circle is on the circumference of up to six surrounding circles of the same diameter. However, the surrounding circles need not be clearly or completely drawn; in fact, some ancient symbols that are claimed as examples of the Flower of Life contain only a single circle or hexagon. Possibly five patterns resembling the Flower of Life can be seen on one of the granite columns and a further five on a column opposite of the building. They are drawn in red ochre and some are very faint and hard to distinguish.

Painted images of the "flower of life"

Despite claims that they are over 6,000 years old and may date back to as long ago as 10,500 BC or earlier, recent research shows that these symbols can be no earlier than 535 BC, and most probably date to the 2nd and 4th century AD, based on photographic evidence of Greek text, still to be fully deciphered, seen alongside the *flower of life* circles and the position of the circles close to the top of one of the columns, which are over 4 meters in height. (26) This suggests the Osirion was half filled with sand prior to the circles being drawn and therefore likely to have been well after the end of the Ptolemaic dynasty. As the drawings are not mentioned in the extensive listings of graffiti at the temple compiled by Margaret Murray in 1904 it even cannot be excluded that the drawings were added in the 20th century AD. And based on personal observations by Stephen

Mehler, myself and others in April of 2014 with the Khemit School these drawings are indeed surface paintings done in red ochre, and not etched in by a laser or any other fanciful notion.

9/ Karnak

The Karnak Temple Complex, commonly known as Karnak, comprises a vast mix of decayed temples, chapels, pylons, and other buildings. Building at the complex began during the reign of Senusret I in the Middle Kingdom and continued into the Ptolemaic period, although most of the extant buildings date from the New Kingdom. Approximately thirty pharaohs contributed to the buildings, enabling it to reach a size, complexity, and diversity not seen elsewhere. Few of the individual features of Karnak are unique, but the size and number of features are overwhelming. The deities represented range from some of the earliest worshipped to those worshipped much later in the history of the Ancient Egyptian culture.

Stephen at the entrance to Karnak

The ruler Hatshepsut (1508–1458 BC) had monuments constructed here and also restored the original Precinct of Mut, the ancient great goddess of Egypt, that had been ravaged by the foreign rulers during the Hyksos occupation. It is believed by most Egyptologists that she had twin obelisks, at the time the tallest in the world and made of Aswan granite, erected at the entrance to the temple. One still stands, as the tallest surviving ancient obelisk on Earth; the other has broken in two and toppled. Also, it is believed that the unfinished obelisk at Aswan was also commissioned by her. However, as we have already seen in previous parts of this book, the Egyptians at that time did not have iron or steel tools in order to be able to extract large blocks of stone from the Aswan quarry such as the obelisks at Karnak, nor be able to transport or shape them to the high degree that we can even see today. The inscriptions on the granite obelisks were not necessarily engraved when the obelisks were made, but could have been done much later.

Massive rose granite obelisk at Karnak

The nearby massive temples are of course engineering wonders, such as the Hypostyle Hall in the Precinct of Amun-Re, a hall area of 50,000 sq ft (5,000 m2) with 134 massive columns arranged in 16 rows. 122 of these columns are 10 meters tall, and the other 12 are 21 meters tall with a diameter of over three meters. However, the columns, though vast in size, are comprised in sections, whereas the obelisk is one piece of stone, and taller. It is quite likely that the obelisks were the product of an earlier and more technically advanced culture, such as the Khemitians, and were later recycled by leaders such as Hatshepsut.

Gary Evans posing in front of the columns

Something perhaps even more curious, and off in a side area of one of the smaller temples is what appears to be a broken section of a black granite obelisk. Although some may say that its cracked and crumbling appearance is the result of thousands of years of environmental exposure or defacement, it confounded engineers and geologists that we showed it to both in April 2013 and April 2014. Some with us remarked that the cracks in the surface are so wide that it is as if the stone actually shrank, and that the size of the stone grains in the core became larger than on the exterior. The reigning hypothesis from our groups is that energy appears to have been transmitted through the stone, and then a high energetic pulse caused destabilization of the material; in essence, *frying* it.

Yousef and others and the curious erosion

Geologist Suzan puzzled by the strange black granite

The Egyptian word for obelisk "tekhen" meant "to pierce" and it is thought that the obelisk symbolically pierced the sky. The Khemit School prefer the ancient name *Ib Ra,* which means "a beam from the heart of the Sun" Obelisks are often connected with the Sun, and ancient authors saw its design as a representation of the sun's rays. As markers at the front of temples, obelisks served to demarcate the religious world of the gods from the secular world outside. Many obelisks also were erected to praise pharaohs for battlefield victories, and as such they are an embodiment of the connection between the divine and earthly power of pharaohs. (27) Of course, the shape of obelisks is often thought to be phallic in nature.

The idea that these obelisks were created on behalf of the rulers of Egypt to commemorate themselves and their accomplishments is of course the common belief of most Egyptologists, however, none to my knowledge has been able to logically describe how these massive precise forms were quarried, moved and shaped with the tools that we know the ancient Egyptians had. Just because an obelisk has an inscription of a pharaoh's life on it or that of many rulers does not mean that the writing and the obelisk are contemporary. We shall see, especially in the case of the large stone boxes located in the Serapeum at Saqqara, that the quality of the inscription is often far inferior than the precision of the obelisk's surface.

Although I have not been able to find any literature on the hypothesis, the damage to the black granite obelisk section may have been the result of an energetic overload, if we presume that the original function of some of the obelisks were made prior to dynastic times, and were later adopted by the pharaohs. As we have already seen, examples of works created using lost ancient high technology are abundant in Egypt, and the obelisks could be examples of that; not originally ornaments, but parts of an energy network. We will get much more into that further along in the book, especially when we discuss the Giza plateau and its pyramids. According to engineer Chris Dunn and others, the Great pyramid and others in the area may have been power plants of some sort, and if this is true, then the obelisks may have been energy receivers. Tesla type wireless technology thousands of years before Tesla existed.

Remnant of a rose granite obelisk seemingly tuned to a specific frequency

Possible evidence that the obelisks were originally energetic resonators is the fact that the broken one seen in the above photo when struck with a fist emits a very specific and repeatable audible frequency. This could mean that each one was created for a specific tone, and that is why the unfinished obelisk in the Aswan quarry was abandoned once the large crack was detected. Rather than simply cut it into smaller pieces, or make one obelisk slightly smaller than the original specifications, the original builders simply moved on to another project one would presume.

Other examples of unexplained technology at Karnak include drill cores. They are largely or even wholly overlooked by most academics and tour guides; either because they do not see them, or would not know what to say when pressed for answers as to how they were made. The massive one in the following photos is not the only one at Karnak, but is the largest. As you can see, only a portion of the core is still present; the rest having broken off in antiquity, or possibly recently.

The wall of the presumed core drill would have been less than 3 mm in diameter; a feat that we would perhaps be hard pressed to replicate today.

Massive tube drill hole in rose Aswan granite

Close up of the large drill hole

In order to cut through the Aswan granite in this example and others that you will see, the bit itself must be harder than the quartz crystal of Mohs scale 7 hardness that makes up a high percentage of this granite, and the common core drills used today are diamond coated to achieve this. The key technology of the diamond drill is the actual diamond bit itself. It is composed of industrial diamonds set into a soft metallic matrix. As shown in the figure below, the diamonds are scattered throughout the matrix, and the action relies on the matrix to slowly wear during the drilling, so as to expose more diamonds. The bit is mounted onto a drill stem, which is connected to a rotary drill. Water is injected into the drill pipe, so as to wash out the rock cuttings produced by the bit and also to reduce the heat produced due to friction which causes less wear and tear of the bits. An actual diamond bit is a complex affair, usually designed for a specific rock type, with many channels for washing. (28)

Modern core drill with embedded diamond abrasive

Does this sound like a technology that the dynastic Egyptians had? There are of course some that will say that such core drilling is recent, but cannot explain why the Egyptian government would allow such activity in one of their sacred and popular tourist sites. Also, a very powerful electric drill would be required to achieve this, and many fine examples of core drilling can be seen at sites such as Abu Sir, which we will discuss later. Abu Sir is at least half a kilometer away from any electrical outlet.

Just one of many drill holes at Karnak

10/ Meidum

The pyramid at Meidum is thought to originally have been built for Huni, the last pharaoh of the Third Dynasty, and was continued, supposedly, by Sneferu. The architect was a successor to the famous Imhotep, regarded by Egyptologists as the inventor of the stone built pyramid. Most Egyptologists believe that the collapse of the pyramid is likely due to the modifications made to Imhotep's pyramid design as well as the decisions taken twice during construction to extend the pyramid.

The main pyramid at Meidum

The second extension turned the original step pyramid design into a true pyramid by filling in the steps with limestone encasing. While this approach is consistent with the design of the other true pyramids, Meidum was supposedly affected by construction errors. Firstly, the outer layer was founded on sand and not on rock, like the inner layers, which would be a major oversight by the engineers.

Secondly, the inner step pyramids had been designed as the final stage. Thus the outer surface was polished and the platforms of the steps were not horizontal, but fell off to the outside. This severely compromised the stability and is likely to have caused the collapse of the Meidum Pyramid in a downpour while the building was still under construction. (29)

Some believe the pyramid not to have collapsed until the New Kingdom, but there are a number of facts contradicting this theory. The Meidum Pyramid seems never to have been completed. Beginning with Sneferu and to the 12th dynasty all pyramids had a valley temple, which is missing at Meidum. However, the idea that it was quarried could be a possibility. The mortuary temple, which was found under the rubble at the base of the pyramid, apparently never was finished. Two Steles inside, usually bearing the names of the pharaoh, are missing inscriptions. The burial chamber inside the pyramid itself is uncompleted, with raw walls and wooden supports still in place which are usually removed after construction. However, this could have been the result of later attempts at reconstruction.

Passage leading down into the pyramid core at Meidum

First chamber inside the Meidum pyramid

The first room you enter after descending the passageway may have been left unfinished due to the pyramid at least partially collapsing. What is astonishing is the level of craftsmanship as seen in the following photos.

Seamless mortar free construction

There is no mortar whatsoever in the joints of the limestone blocks, and any gaps seen in the above photo are the result of the material having broken off due to the presumed earlier catastrophic event.

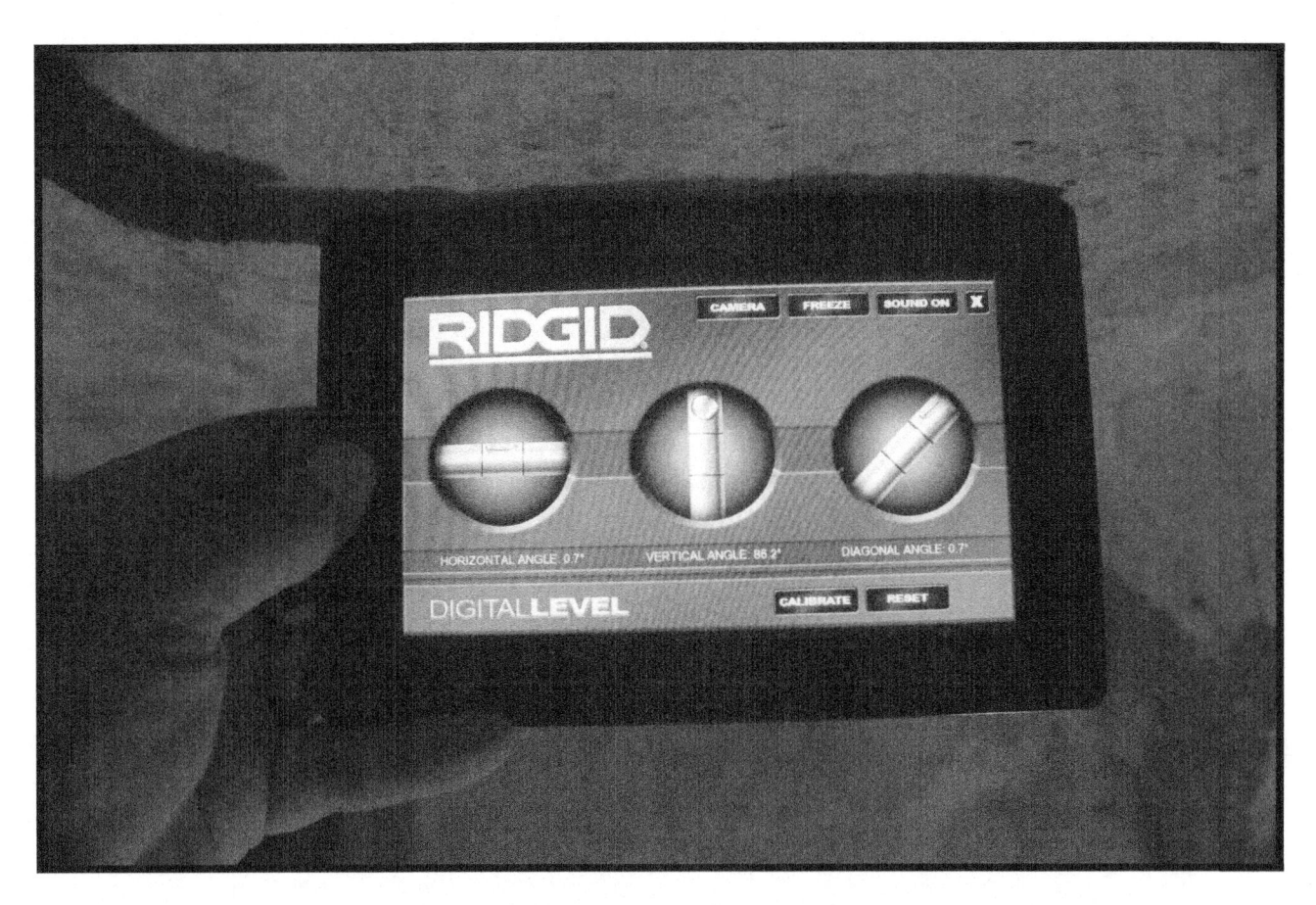

Astonishing level of accuracy

What really shocked was the ceiling of this chamber. As the above photo shows, it was within 0.7 degrees of being perfectly level, and in some areas even closer to 0.0. Would the pyramid builders really have gone to that much trouble?

Richard, Gary and others toning

Deeper into the pyramid and up a series of installed modern staircases is a chamber, presumably to be the final resting place of the pharaoh. The major question is why is it not simply a cube shaped room, instead of having this stepped design to the walls? What we will see is that this phenomenon occurs in many of the ancient pyramids from Meidum north to those at the Giza Plateau. The individuals in the above photo, guided by Gary Evans on the right spent some time chanting inside this room, and their sound seemed to become greatly amplified when they hit specific tones. Would the great builders have done this intentionally if it was the tomb of a dead leader, and leave the walls bare of any painting, or carved in hieroglyphics? Or was the resonance aspect part of the design, because the pyramid itself was built as a resonating energetic structure? This avenue of thought we will explore at length once we get to the Giza Plateau later on in the book.

Affiliated mastabas were never used or completed and none of the usual burials have been found. Finally, the first examinations of the Meidum Pyramid found everything below the surface of the rubble mound fully intact. Stones from the outer cover were stolen only after they were exposed by the excavations. This makes a catastrophic collapse more probable than a gradual one. And that is indeed what I observed when I entered into the inner chambers of the pyramid as the photos show. One can't honestly date when the damage to the pyramid occurred. If you presume that the initial construction of this massive structure was done during the time of Snerferu, then that would date t to a very narrow time frame. However, based on the amazing precision of the stone work, is it possible that the pyramid is much older, and the product of perhaps the pre-dynastic Khemitians?

Mud brick over megalithic stone excellence

As you can see in the above photo, mud brick walls stand above a far more elegant and difficult to construct mortar free stone floor. Are we not taught that cultures tend to evolve as regards their technical abilities?

Growing evidence suggests that a cataclysm occurred approximately 12,000 years ago that affected the entire planet, and may have led to damage and destruction in Egypt as well. In the 1950s, Immanuel Velikovsky propounded catastrophism in several popular books. He speculated that the planet Venus is a former "comet" which was ejected from Jupiter and subsequently 3,500 years ago made two catastrophic close passes by Earth, 52 years apart, and later interacted with Mars, which then had a series of near collisions with Earth which ended in 687 B.C., before settling into its current orbit. Velikovsky used this to explain the biblical plagues of Egypt, the biblical reference to the "Sun standing still" for a day (from the biblical book of Joshua 10:12 & 13, explained by changes in Earth's rotation), and the sinking of Atlantis. Scientists rejected Velikovsky's theories, often quite passionately. (30)

Almost fifty years later, in 1997 authors D.S. Allan and J.B. Delair published their book "Cataclysm!" Using more powerful analytical tools, they looked at the data Velikovsky examined and proposed a fresh thesis of their own. Like Velikovsky, they believed that folklore myths were eyewitness reports of what was seen in the sky. They described many of the myths Velikovsky described and added more that were unavailable to Velikovsky. From their research, they concluded that a fragment of an exploding supernova entered our solar system around 9500 B.C. This fragment "Phaeton-Marduk" caused one of Neptune's moons to become the planet Pluto. Phaeton-Marduk then pulled one of Saturn's moons, Chiron, away from Saturn making it the smallest planet in the Solar System. Chiron was first discovered in 1976. Phaeton-Marduk then caused the fragmentation of the planet Taimat. Taimat's fragments are now the asteroid belts between Jupiter and Mars. Taimat's moon, Kingu, went into orbit around Phaeton-Marduk. Phaeton-Marduk then came close to the Earth disturbing the Earth's rotation. The moon, Kingu, was pulled from Taimat by Earth's gravitation. Kingu fell apart, the pieces plunging into the Earth. These combined disturbances caused the Deluge. Phaeton-Marduk then flipped Venus upside down, causing it to have a backward rotation. Phaeton-Marduk finally fell into the sun. Allan and Delair also described geological data showing large deposits of broken bones and shattered trees mixed together in heaps and data describing lakes that have beds resembling craters that might have been formed by aerial bombardment of huge meteors, and many other geological abnormalities.

Artistic depiction of catastrophic event

Author Barbara Hand Clow examines legendary cataclysms in her 2001 book *Catastrophobia: The Truth Behind Earth Changes* (now called *Awakening The Planetary Mind)* and shows how, contrary to many prophecies of doom; we are actually on the cusp of an era of incredible creative growth. The recent discovery of the remains of ancient villages buried beneath the Black Sea is the latest instance of mounting evidence that many of the "mythic" catastrophes of history such as the fall of Atlantis and the Biblical Flood were actual events. She shows that a series of cataclysmic disasters, caused by a massive disturbance in the Earth's crust 11,500 years ago, rocked the world and left humanity's collective psyche deeply scarred. Her inspirations for writing this book were Allan and Delair as well as the oral traditions taught to her from her Native Cherokee grandfather.

From Hand Clow's perspective we are a wounded species, and this unprocessed fear, passed from generation to generation, is responsible for our constant expectations of apocalypse, from Y2K to the famed end of the Mayan calendar in 2012.

In her expanded edition of *Catastrophobia,* entitled *Awakening the Planetary Mind: Beyond the Trauma of the Past to a New Era of Creativity* she discusses further the mounting geological and archaeological evidence that many of these mythic catastrophes were actual events, and further reveals the existence of a highly advanced global maritime culture that disappeared amid great earth changes and rising seas 14,000 to 11,500 years ago, nearly causing our species' extinction. It was first published in 2011.

Physicist Paul LaViolette wrote the compelling *Earth Under Fire: Humanity's Survival of the Ice Age* in 2005 which demonstrates how ancient myths and lore have preserved an accurate record of a missing era in human history, and are not simply the fantasies of cultures of the past. Compelled by his decryption of an ancient warning hidden in zodiac constellation lore, LaViolette worked with information from many scientific sources, including astronomical observations, polar ice core measurements, and other geological data, to confirm that our galaxy's core exploded, unleashing a barrage of cosmic rays that arrived near the end of the last ice age. This barrage caused the solar system to become enveloped in a dense nebula, which led to periods of persistent darkness, frigid cold, severe solar storms, searing heat, and mountainous floods that plagued mankind for many generations. Linking his scientific findings to details preserved in ancient myths and monuments, he demonstrates how past civilizations accurately recorded the causes of these cataclysmic events, from his 1983 doctoral thesis about the Galactic Superwave.

In this theory, LaViolette hypothesizes that galactic core outbursts are the most energetic phenomenon taking place in the universe. During the early 60's astronomers began to realize that the massive object that forms the core of a spiral or giant elliptical galaxy periodically becomes active spewing out a fierce barrage of cosmic rays with a total energy output equal to hundreds of thousands of supernova explosions. (31)

During the 70's astronomers realized that the core of our own Galaxy (the Milky Way) has also had a history of recurrent outbursts, that at periodic intervals it enters an active phase in which its rate of cosmic ray emission rises many orders of magnitude. (32) According to LaViolette, galactic core explosions actually occur about every 13,000 to 26,000 years for major outbursts and more frequently for lesser events. The emitted cosmic rays escape from the core virtually unimpeded. As they travel radially outward through the Galaxy, they form a spherical shell that advances at very close to the speed of light. The last major outburst, based on a study of astronomical and geological data reveals that a super wave from our Galactic core impacted our solar system near the end of the last ice age, 11,000 to 16,000 years ago. (33)

Also, Dr. Robert Schoch, professor at Boston University in the United States authored the book *Forgotten Civilization: The Role of Solar Outbursts in Our Past and Future* published in 2012 where he briefly recaps his two decades of work on the Great Sphinx of Egypt, but more importantly presents his latest research centred on the magnificent Göbekli Tepe complex in Turkey, which confirms his thesis that ancient civilization goes back thousands of years earlier than mainstream historians generally care to acknowledge. Also presented is a new discovery: a reinterpretation of the mysterious rongorongo texts of Easter Island, as the glyphs connect to the work of a prominent plasma physicist. He discusses how solar outbursts and plasma discharges brought about the rapid end of the last ice age and the demise of the early civilizations of that remote period. And in terms of time frame, Schoch believes that the last ice age ended abruptly in 9700 BC, as in 11,700 years ago due to coronal mass ejections from the sun.

Possible example of stone vitrification in Peru

What Allan and Delair, Hand Clow, De LaViolette and Schoch all have in common, aside from describing a major catastrophic event that happened in the past, is when this occurred, around 11,500 to 12,000 years ago. If they had differing dates, separated by thousands of years, then we would not be looking at a cohesive theory, but we are.

Whether it was a meteor or other celestial body striking the earth, a close pass by a comet, or an energy eruption from galactic center or the sun, the result would have been devastating. Perhaps the most obvious result of this cataclysmic event, which has been well documented, is the so called Holocene extinction of large animals, especially in North America which occurred beginning around 12,000 years ago.

Woolly mammoth, victim of a cataclysm

So what is proposed here is of course radical, but is backed up by serious researchers, such as those noted above. If such a massive catastrophic event was indeed global, any ancient people, whether advanced or primitive, would have been affected. In the case of Egypt, this may explain why Egyptologists are basically at a loss for words, or at least logical explanations, when they try to explain how the unfinished obelisk of Aswan, giant statues at the Ramesseum and Memnon, core drill holes, and many other examples of lost ancient high technology we shall look at were achieved by the bronze age dynastic Egyptians.

The mystery of course is who the great builders were. As far as I can tell, only the works of Stephen Mehler and the Khemit School based on the knowledge of Abd'El Hakim Awyan fits the bill. The only evidence that remains are the stone works themselves and the oral traditions that explain who the Khemitians were. Most academics, especially Egyptologists scoff at the idea that an advanced ancient civilization existed in Egypt prior to about 3100 BC, let alone 9,500 BC, but as we progress through the landscape and artifacts, hopefully a logical pattern will emerge.

11/ Dashur

Dashur is a royal necropolis located in the desert on the west bank of the Nile approximately 40 kilometres (25 mi) south of Cairo. It is known chiefly for several pyramids, two of which are among the oldest, largest and best preserved in Egypt, and according to most Egyptologists they were built from 2613 to 2589 BC.

The Bent Pyramid and the Red Pyramid are thought by most Egyptologists to have been constructed during the reign of Pharaoh Sneferu (2613 to 2589 BC), father of Khufu of the Old Kingdom. The shape of the Bent Pyramid is unique; it represents what many scholars believe is a transitional pyramid form to have been the result of an engineering crisis encountered during its construction. The Red Pyramid is called the world's first true smooth sided pyramid, while the Black Pyramid dates from the later reign of Amenemhat III and, although badly eroded, it remains the most imposing monument at the site after the two "Sneferu" pyramids.

Khemit School at the Bent Pyramid

The Bent Pyramid's lower part rises from the desert at a 54 degree inclination, but the top section is built at the shallower angle of 43 degrees, lending the pyramid its very obvious "bent" appearance. Egyptologists believe that the Bent Pyramid represents a transitional form between step sided and smooth sided pyramids such as that of Meidum. It has been suggested that due to the steepness of the original angle of inclination the structure may have begun to show signs of instability during construction, forcing the builders to adopt a shallower angle to avert the structure's collapse. (34) This theory appears to be borne out, according to the Egyptologists by the fact that the adjacent Red Pyramid, built immediately afterwards, they contend, and supposedly by the same Pharaoh, was constructed at an angle of 43 degrees from its base. This fact also contradicts the theory that at the initial angle the construction would take too long because Sneferu's death was nearing, so the builders changed the angle to complete the construction in time.

Amazing precision of the casing stones

The casing stone, which is surprisingly intact aside from the corners, shows an amazing degree of precision, as the photo above shows. In comparison, the inner core looks as if it were not as well made. The stones are more loosely fitting, and the photo below shows possible evidence of ancient concrete used to fill in the spaces. Whether this mortar is part of the additional construction or some later repair is impossible to say.

Inner stones of the Bent Pyramid with traces of concrete

Amazing accuracy of the casing stones

Also, the casing stone, which was not simply applied to the exterior of the pyramid but interlocks with the core stones, is remarkably level. In the photo above you can see that in some cases it is 0.3 degrees from being perfectly level.

A very curious point is that only the corners of the pyramid are missing their casing stones. Many Egyptologists of course believe that later people used the structure as a quarry, and simply attacked the corners because they presumably would be the easiest to get at. But harvest all four corners relatively evenly? And not simply work away at one, then move left and right removing the stone as you go? Another theory is that this pyramid was part of a massive energy network, with those at Giza perhaps being the epicenter. An overload of this energy system, possibly resulting from the great global catastrophe of about 12,000 years ago could have caused explosions inside the pyramids, resulting in much of the damage we see today. This concept will be explored much more when we explore the Giza Plateau.

The Red Pyramid, also called the North Pyramid, is the largest of the three major pyramids located at the Dashur necropolis. Named for the rusty reddish hue of its iron rich limestone core stones, it is also the third largest Egyptian pyramid, after the so called Khufu and Khafre at Giza, if you believe the conventional time line of Egyptologists. At the time of its completion, it was theoretically the tallest man made structure in the world. The Red Pyramid was not always red. It used to be cased with white Tura limestone, but only a few of these stones now remain at the pyramid's base, at the corner. During the Middle Ages much of the white Tura limestone was taken for buildings in Cairo, revealing the durable reddish limestone beneath.

The Red Pyramid devoid of casing stones

Egyptologists disagree on the length of time it took to construct. Based on quarry marks found at various phases of construction, Rainer Stadelmann estimates the time of completion to be approximately 17 years while John Romer, based on this same information, suggests it took only ten years and seven months to build. This is presuming that you believe that it and the other two pyramids were constructed during the time of Sneferu. (35) The Red Pyramid is 105 metres (344 ft) high. A rare pyramidion, or capstone, for the Red Pyramid has been uncovered and reconstructed, and is now on display at Dashur. However, whether it was actually ever used is unclear, as its angle of inclination differs from that of the pyramid it was apparently intended for. This pyramid along with the Bent Pyramid was closed to tourists for many years because of a nearby army camp. It is now usually open for tourists and somewhat intrusive ventilation has been installed which pipes air down the entrance shaft to the interior chambers.

Khemit School entering the Red Pyramid

Descending passage into the core of the Red Pyramid

Inside the first of the three chambers

There are 3 chambers or rooms inside the Red Pyramid. As you can see in the above photo the passage connecting chambers one and two is very small, and thus if the rooms were for funerary purposes no large objects could be moved from one into the other, and the descending passage is also very restrictive. And yet, as we saw with the pyramid at Meidum, all three of the chambers have high corbelled ceilings, respond to specific chanted frequencies and have no inscriptions what so ever.

Suzan and Tony pondering the acoustics

Are we really to believe that the Bent and Red were made during the rule of Sneferu, and that his engineers were so incompetent that they wasted the nation's resources experimenting on the first one being the Bent Pyramid, full scale, and having blundered both the proper angle and also stability of the structure had to abandon it?

Personally, I prefer the view of Stephen Mehler and Khemit School, who claim that "Seneferu" (not Sneferu) was the name given to the Bent Pyramid, as Seneferu may mean "double harmony" in the ancient Suf language of Egypt. Both of these structures according to the now deceased figure head of the Khemit School, Abd'El Hakim Awyan predate the dynastic Egyptians by thousands of years and were later inherited by the Pharaohs. Since they would have clearly been in awe of the works of earlier people, the area was used as a cemetery by high ranking people during dynastic times.

12/ Saqqara

Saqqara also spelled Sakkara or Saccara in English, is a vast, ancient burial ground in Egypt, serving as the necropolis for the Ancient Egyptian capital, Memphis (36) as well as for the later Greeks and Romans. The area features numerous pyramids, including the world famous Step pyramid of Djoser, sometimes referred to as the Step Tomb due to its rectangular base, as well as a number of mastabas (Arabic word meaning 'bench'). It is located some 30 km (19 mi) south of modern-day Cairo, and covers an area of around 7 by 1.5 km (4.35 by 0.93 mi) making it one of the largest archaeological sites in the world.

The Djoser Pyramid at Saqqara

At Saqqara, the allegedly oldest complete stone building complex known in history exists; Djoser's step pyramid, said to have been built by Egyptologists during the third dynasty. Another 16 Egyptian kings built pyramids at Saqqara, which are now in various states of preservation or dilapidation. High officials also added private funeral monuments to this necropolis during the entire **pharaohnic period**. It remained an important complex as well for non-royal burials and cult ceremonies for more than 3,000 years, well into **Ptolemaic** and **Roman** times. North of the area known as Saqqara we find **Abusir** and south **Dashur**, which we have just covered.

Contrary to popular belief, the name Saqqara is not derived from the ancient Egyptian funerary god **Sokar**, but from the **Beni Saqqar** who are a local Berber tribe. (36) Their name means "Sons of Saqqar." Since they are not indigenous to the area it would not follow that they would fashion themselves as being born of an ancient Egyptian god whose identity was unknown until the age of archaeology. As well, it must be remembered that most of the ancient Egyptian sites' names are Arabic, and not ancient Egyptian.

The earliest known burials of nobles can be traced back to the **First Dynasty**, at the north side of the Saqqara plateau. During this time, the royal burial ground was at **Abydos**. The first royal burials at Saqqara, comprising underground galleries, are dated by Egyptologists to the **Second Dynasty**. The last Second Dynasty king **Khasekhemwy** was buried in his tomb at Abydos, but also possibly built a funerary monument at Saqqara consisting of a large rectangular enclosure, known as **Gisr el-Mudir**. It probably inspired the monumental enclosure wall around the Step Pyramid complex. Djoser's funerary complex, built by the royal architect **Imhotep**, further comprises a large number of dummy buildings and a secondary mastaba (the so called "Southern Tomb.") French architect and Egyptologist **Jean-Philippe Lauer** spent the greater part of his life excavating and restoring Djoser's funerary complex.

One of the proposed Khemitian works at Saqqara

However, some, such as Stephen Mehler, Yousef Awyan and Mohammed Ibrahim of the Khemit School insist that some of the structures, especially those of fine limestone at Saqqara predate the dynastic Egyptians, and are the remains of works done by the more ancient Khemitians. Of particular note is what Hakim called the "teaching hospital" or "hospital" which was used in Khemitian times for diagnosis and treatment of illness using acoustics. They also contend that the fact that the smooth limestone surface was coated with a wax compound would have further enhanced sound or other vibrations used in the healing processes.

Another presumed Khemitian work at Saqqara

Unfortunately, these beautiful limestone edifices have been victims of later people who once again deconstructed them, at least partially for other building projects, either at Saqqara, or further afield.

Nearly all Fourth Dynasty kings are said to have chosen to have a different location for their pyramids. During the second half of the Old Kingdom, under the Fifth and Sixth Dynasties, Saqqara was again the royal burial ground. The Fifth and Sixth Dynasty pyramids are not built of massive stone, but with a core consisting of rubble. They are consequently less well preserved than the world famous pyramids said to have been built by the Fourth Dynasty kings at Giza. Unas, or Wenis, the last ruler of the Fifth Dynasty, was the first king to adorn the chambers in his pyramid with the now famous Pyramid Texts. It was custom for courtiers during the Old Kingdom to be buried in mastaba tombs close to the pyramid of their king. Clusters of private tombs were thus formed in Saqqara around the pyramid complexes of Unas and Teti.

From the Middle Kingdom onwards, Memphis was no longer the capital of the country, and kings built their funerary complexes elsewhere. Few private monuments from this period have been found at Saqqara. During the New Kingdom Memphis was an important administrative and military centre, second only to the capital. From the Eighteenth Dynasty onwards many high officials built tombs at Saqqara. When still a general, Horemheb built a large tomb here, though he was later buried as Pharaoh in the Valley of the Kings at Thebes. Other important tombs belong to the vizier Aperel and to Maya. Most Egyptologists believe that Maya was the Overseer of the Treasury during the reign of Pharaoh Tutankhamun, Ay and Horemheb of the eighteenth dynasty. He was also an important official and was noted for restoring the burials of several earlier Pharaohs in the Royal Necropolis in the years following the deaths of Tutankhamun and Ay.

However, Stephen Mehler, based on his discussions with Abd'El Hakim Awyan believes that Maya actually refers to a person of Central American Mayan ancestry, as evidenced by the symbols painted on the ceiling inside the small temple. Upon consulting with Mayan wisdom keeper Humbatsmen, and then later with the latter's spiritual teacher Don Alejandro, the two Mayan mystics stated that what Mehler had shown them was in fact ancient glyph work of their culture. This could mean that visitations by Native American people occurred during dynastic times; an idea which most Egyptologists probably shun.

Glyphs interpreted to be from the Mayan culture

Another intriguing discovery on our 2014 trip to Saqqara was the discovery, by Yousef Awyan of an inscription in a chamber near the Titi Pyramid which Stephen Mehler interpreted to say "The direction from Tawy (Khemit) to Per-Oo (many houses) is across 5 waters."

Yousef expresses his glee at interpreting "Peru"

The three rectangles seen in the photo above are the symbols for house, which is *Per* in the ancient and pre-dynastic Suf language of Egypt. *Per* by itself, as in one symbol by itself means "one house" while two of these symbols together mean, of course, two houses, or *Peri*. When you have three or more of them together you have *Peru*, or "many houses." Although the vocal sound *Peru* does not necessarily mean that it refers to the country of Peru, however, most people, including Peruvians themselves do not know where that name comes from. According to scholars I have spoken with in the Cusco area, home of the Inca, Peru is a very ancient name for the highlands of what we call Peru today, when the first advanced society lived there, who were called the *Peruhas,* or *Piruhas.*

Many monuments from earlier periods were still standing at Saqqara during the 18th Dynasty, but dilapidated by this period. Prince **Khaemweset**, son of Pharaoh **Ramesses II**, made repairs to buildings at Saqqara. Among other things, he restored the **Pyramid of Unas** and added an inscription to its south face to commemorate the restoration. He enlarged the Serapeum, the proposed burial site of the mummified Apis bulls, and was later buried in the catacombs. The Serapeum, supposedly containing one undisturbed interment of an Apis bull and the tomb of Khaemweset, were rediscovered by the French Egyptologist Auguste Mariette.

Gary on top of one of the boxes in the Serapeum

However, the boxes in the Serapeum are examples of what engineers such as Chris Dunn, I, and members of the Khemit School have major problems with as regards the conventional Egyptologists' explanations. According to the latter, in the 13th century BC, Khaemweset ordered that a tunnel be excavated through the solid limestone bedrock, with side chambers designed to contain large granite sarcophagi weighing at least 70 tonnes each, to hold the mummified remains of the bulls. (37) The temple was discovered by Auguste Mariette, who had gone to Egypt to collect Coptic manuscripts but later grew interested in the remains of the Saqqara necropolis. In 1850, Mariette found the head of one sphinx sticking out of the shifting desert sand dunes, cleared the sand, and followed the boulevard to the site. After using explosives to clear rocks blocking the entrance to the catacomb, he excavated most of the complex. (38) Unfortunately, his notes of the excavation were lost, which has complicated the use of these burials in establishing Egyptian chronology. Mariette found one undisturbed burial, which is supposedly now at the Agricultural Museum in Cairo. The other 26 sarcophagi, of the bulls, had been "robbed."

Sense of scale of the stone boxes in the Serapeum

The question obviously arises as to who would want to steal mummified bulls. Aside from the fact that they would be large and cumbersome to remove from the sealed Serapeum boxes, whose lids weigh more than 10 tons, would they have been covered in gold or contain precious stones that would make the process of plundering worthwhile? It seems more likely that since Mariette presumed that all of the boxes once contained mummified bulls, he was speculating that they had been stolen; not a scientific idea that holds any water.

Manufacturing Chris Dunn is a man who knows what precision surfaces look like, as he has been involved in making complex metal parts for the aviation industry for decades. He has studied the boxes in the Serapeum many times, and has been able to measure the flatness of their granite and limestone surfaces using precise gauges. The following are his thoughts, as found in an article on his website *www.gizapower.com*:

The granite box inside Khafre's pyramid has the same characteristics as the boxes inside the Serapeum. Yet the boxes in the Serapeum were ascribed to the 18th dynasty, over 1100 years later when stone working was supposedly in decline. Considering that this dating was based on pottery items that were found and not the boxes themselves, it would be reasonable to speculate that the boxes have not been dated accurately. Their characteristics show that their creators used the same tools and were blessed with the same skill and knowledge as those who created Khafre's pyramid. Moreover, the boxes in both locations are evidence of a much higher purpose than mere burial sarcophagi. They are finished to a high accuracy; their corners are remarkably square, and their inside corners worked down to a dimension that is sharper than what one would expect to find in an artifact from prehistory. All of these features are extremely difficult to accomplish and none of them necessary for a mere burial box.

Yousef reading the glyphs on one of the boxes

The manufacturers of these boxes in the Serapeum not only created inside surfaces that were flat when measured vertically and horizontally, they also made sure that the surfaces they were creating were square and parallel to each other, with one surface, the top, having sides that are 5 feet and 10 feet apart from each other. But without such parallism and squareness of the top surface, the squareness noted on both sides would not exist.

While it may be argued that modern man cannot impose a modern perspective on artifact that are thousands of years old, an appreciation of the level of precision found in these artifacts is lacking in archaeological literature and is only revealed by an understanding what it takes to produce this kind of work. As an engineer and craftsman, who has worked in manufacturing for over 40 years and who has created precision artifacts in our modern world, in my opinion this accomplishment in prehistory deserves more recognition. Nobody does this kind of work unless there is a very high purpose for the artifact. Even the concept of this kind of precision does not occur to an artisan unless there is no other means of accomplishing what the artifact is intended to do. The only other reason that such precision would be created in an object would be that the tools that are used to create it are so precise that they are incapable of producing anything less than precision. With either scenario, we are looking at a higher civilization in prehistory than what is currently accepted. To me, the implications are staggering.

Amazing precise 90 degree angle

This is why I believe that these artifacts that I have measured in Egypt are the smoking gun that proves, without a shadow of a doubt, that a higher civilization than what we have been taught existed in ancient Egypt. The evidence is cut into the stone. (39)

What we also have to take into consideration is that most of the boxes in the Serapeum were made of granite, and most likely stone brought from the quarry at Aswan, about 500 miles from Saqqara. Not only was that, but the lid of each box cut from the same stone as the box itself. Why would the makers go to such trouble if bulls, no matter how prized, were the contents? It would appear, as Dunn alluded to, that the Serapeum boxes were not created in the 18th Dynasty and not by the dynastic Egyptians at all, but are remnants of an older and more technologically sophisticated culture, possibly the Khemitians. What their original function was is unclear, but they were possibly used for some kind of energetic resonance, and that is why it was vital that the box and lid were made of the same piece of stone. The granite from Aswan is, as has been previously stated as much as 55% quartz crystal.

Quartz crystals have piezoelectric properties, meaning that they are capable of changing a mechanical force into electricity, or an electric current into a mechanical force. A slice, or wafer, of quartz crystal will generate an electric current when it is subjected to pressure. Conversely, a wafer connected in an alternating electric circuit will expand and contract, or oscillate, at a fixed frequency. This frequency depends on the thickness of the wafer. Thin wafers oscillate at higher frequencies than thick ones. (40)

We also have to consider that some of the exterior surfaces of the Serapeum boxes have hieroglyphics carved into them, and that is how Egyptologists have dated the age of manufacture of the boxes themselves. However, the quality of the inscriptions is radically inferior to the surfaces of the boxes, and thus could have been added even thousands of years later.

Inferior etching on a superior flat surface

In the Cairo museum and in other museums around the world there are examples of stone ware that were found in and around the step pyramid at Saqqara. Flinders Petrie also found pieces of similar stoneware at Giza. There are several special things about these bowls, vases and plates that must be discussed. They show the unmistakable tool marks of a lathe manufactured item. This can easily be seen in the center of the open bowls or plates where the angle of the cut changes rapidly, leaving a clean, narrow and perfectly circular line made by the tip of the cutting tool. These bowls and stone dishes as well as platters are some of the finest ever found, and they are from the earliest period of ancient Egyptian civilization, possibly pre-dynastic. They are made from a variety of materials, from soft stone, such as alabaster, all the way up the hardness scale to very hard, such as granite, porphyry and diorite. (41)

Hard stone bowl in the museum at Saqqara

Working with soft stone such as alabaster is relatively simple, compared to those such as granite and diorite. Alabaster can be worked with primitive tools and also abrasives such as sand, which of course is abundant in Egypt. The more elegant workings in granite and the other harder stones are a different matter and indicate not only a consummate level of skill, but a different and perhaps more advanced technology. Here is a quote from Petrie himself:

"...the lathe appears to have been as familiar an instrument in the fourth dynasty, as it is in the modern workshops." Here of course he assumes that they were made during that period.

More examples of ancient lathe work

Stoneware such as this has not been found from any later era in Egyptian history and thus it seems that the skills necessary were lost. Some delicate vases are made of very brittle stone such as schist (like a flint) and yet are finished, turned and polished, to a flawless paper thin edge; an extraordinary feat of craftsmanship. Other pieces turned out of granite, porphyry or basalt are fully hollowed with narrow undercut flared openings, and some even have long necks. Since we have yet to reproduce such pieces it is safe to say that the techniques or machinery they employed to produce these bowls has yet to be replicated. There were not just a few of these. Apparently there were thousands found in and around the Step pyramid by Walter Emery in the 1930s. And according to Stephen Mehler, it was old kingdom priests could collect these out of place artifacts from several locations and hid them on purpose in one huge cache.

This hard stone bowl was clearly turned on a lathe

Many of them have inscribed (scratched) onto them the symbols of the earliest rulers of Egypt; the pre-dynastic era monarchs before the pharaohs. Judging by the primitive skill of the inscriptions, it seems unlikely that those signatures were made by the same craftsmen who fashioned the bowls in the first place, as is most likely the case with the Serapeum boxes. Perhaps they were added later by those who had somehow acquired them.

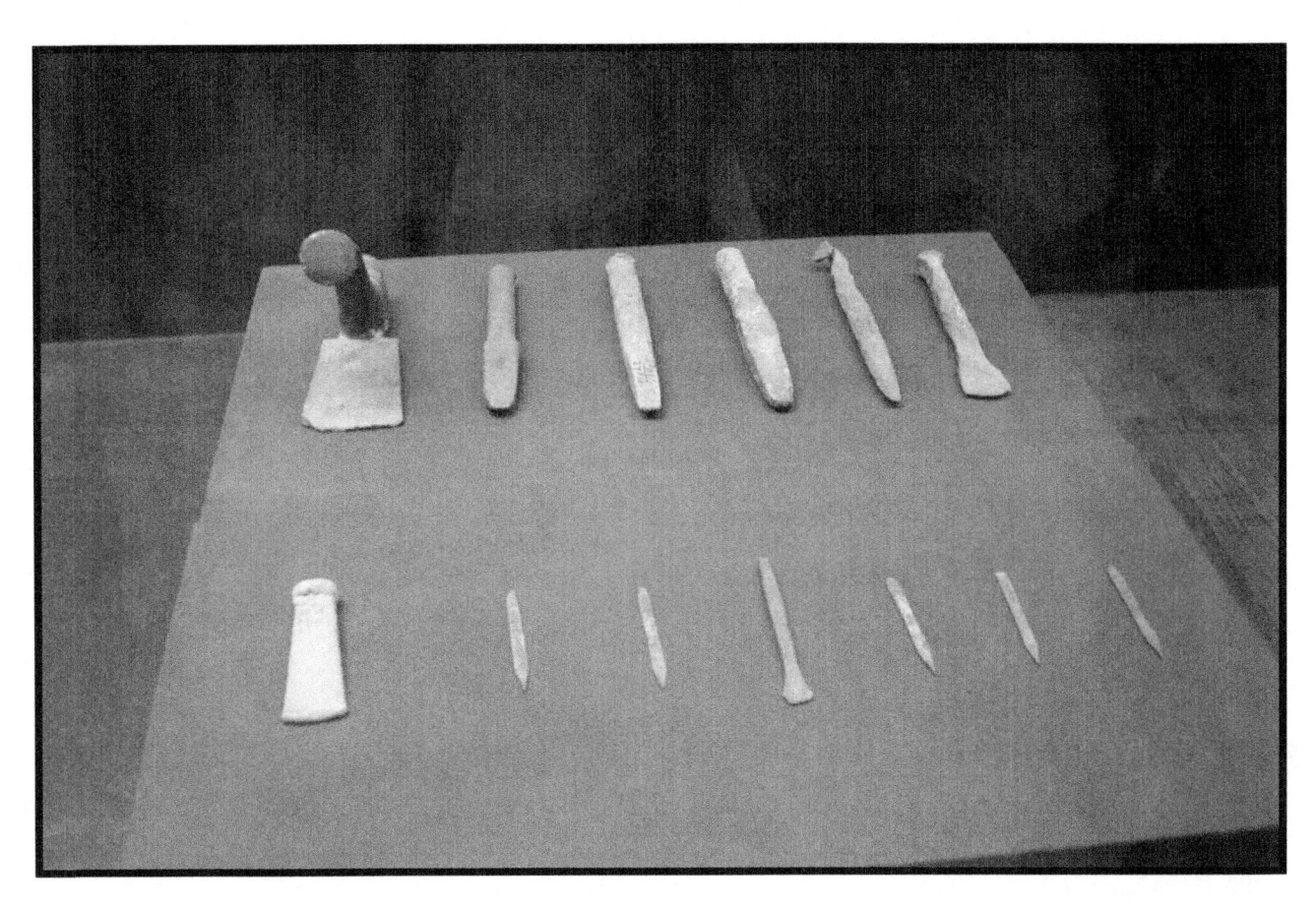

Bronze Dynastic tools in the museum at Saqqara

Lathe turned quartz crystal container in the Petrie Museum in London

Another intriguing artifact, of which there may be several yet only one on display in the Cairo museum is what is called the schist disk. Discovered by Emery in 1936 at Saqqara, the schist disk was uncovered while excavating the tomb of Prince Sabu, the son of Adjuib Pharaoh, governor of the First Dynasty (circa 3,000 BC). While excavating numerous funerary objects from the site, including the stone vessels described above, Emery's attention was drawn to an object that he initially defined in his report on the Great Tombs of the I Dynasty as "a container in the form of schist bowl."

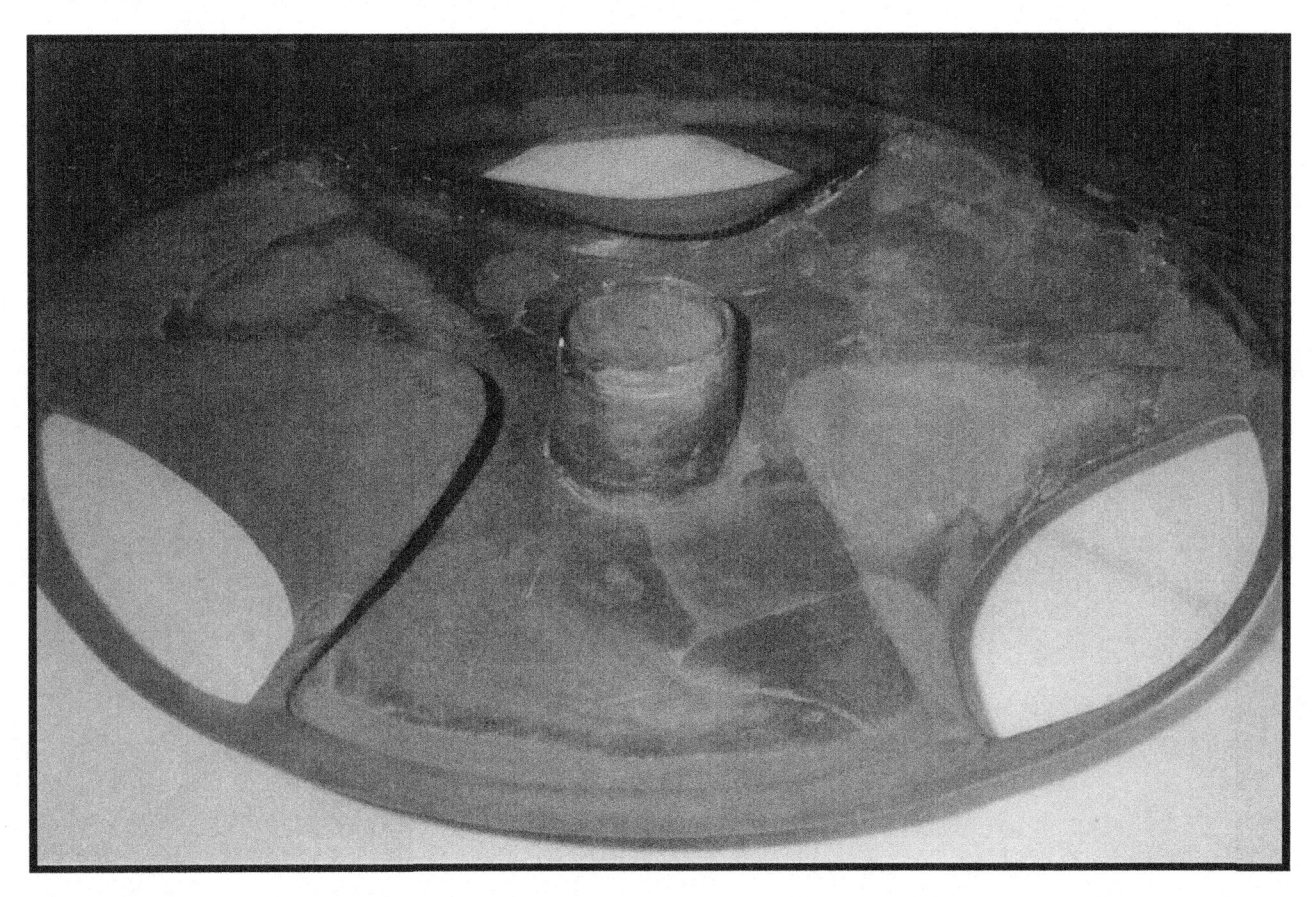

The schist disk in the Cairo Museum

Schists, from the Greek word meaning "to split," (referring to the ease with which this material can be split along the lateral plane), are a category of medium grade metamorphic rocks notable for the preponderance of what are termed "lamellar" minerals such as mica, chlorite, talc, hornblende, and graphite. Derived from clays and muds which have passed through a series of metamorphic processes (involving the production of shales, slates, and phyllites as intermediate steps), most schists are mica, but graphite and chlorite are also widely found. Schist is characteristically foliated, meaning the individual mineral grains split off easily into flakes or slabs.

Approximately 61 cm in diameter (24 inches), one cm thick, and 10.6 cm (4.2 inches) in the center, the Schist Disk was crafted by an unknown means from this very fragile and delicate material requiring very tedious carving, the production of which would confound many artists even today. Resembling a plate or a concave steering wheel of a car, the disk has a series of three cuts or curved "shovels" that resemble the helix of a boat, and in the center, an orifice with a rim that appears to accommodate some axis of a wheel or some other unknown mechanism; conceivably, a central hub designed to fit onto a pole. On display in the first wing of the Egyptian Museum of the Cairo, the Disk is currently labelled an "incense container," although there is no evidence whatsoever to support this assertion. (42)

Another view of the schist disk

Unfortunately there are no high resolution photos of this disk, or any of the other odd artifacts in the Cairo Museum, because taking pictures or video in there is illegal. Whether this "law" is there to protect the artifacts, or simply to inhibit proper study of them is unknown, but I favour the latter reasoning.

While most every archaeologist who has seen the disk feels compelled to offer an opinion as to what purpose the disk served, its futuristic design continues to baffle all who have seen it. Thus, a satisfactory explanation has not yet been provided. Adding to the mystery (and supposition) is the well documented belief that the introduction of the wheel in Egypt didn't occur until the invasion of the Asiatic group known as the Hyksos at the end of the Middle Kingdom, around 1640 BCE. They used it on a number of mechanisms, but primarily on their military chariots.

Other curious objects without descriptions in the Cairo Museum

13/ Abusir

Abusir named "the House or Temple of Osiris" by the ancient Greeks is the name given to an extensive necropolis of the Old Kingdom period, together with later additions, in the vicinity of the modern capital Cairo. The name is also that of a neighbouring village in the Nile Valley, whence the site takes its name, and in present day Egyptian means "Father of Sardines" according to Stephen Mehler; hardly an appropriate name for a site in the desert. Abusir is located several kilometres north of Saqqara and, like it, served as one of the main elite cemeteries for the ancient Egyptian capital city of Memphis. Several other villages in northern and southern Egypt are named Abusir, which according to the Khemit School may have been *Bu Wizzer* or "Land of Osiris."

It is one relatively small segment of the extensive "pyramid field" that extends from north of Giza to below Saqqara, the locality of Abusir took its turn as the focus of the prestigious western burial rites operating out of the then capital of Memphis during the Old Kingdom 5th Dynasty. As an elite cemetery, neighbouring Giza had by then "filled up" with the massive pyramids and other monuments of the 4th Dynasty, leading the 5th Dynasty pharaohs to seek sites elsewhere for their own funerary monuments.

Yousef guiding me through the ruins of Abusir

Abusir is rarely seen by tourists, because it is sometimes made off limits by local authorities for no logical reason, and because it does not have the flash and glamour of the Giza Plateau. It has been ruthlessly quarried over a very long time for its stone, and is, at least on the surface a mere shadow of its former glory. However, if you have a keen eye, and a guide like the one and only Yousef Awyan, there are a remarkable number of astonishing examples of lost ancient high technology that can be found here.

Basalt slab showing clear sign of saw at work

In the photo above Yousef is inspecting a large slab of basalt which was clearly cut with a giant circular saw whose diameter we calculated at being 6 to 8 meters, or 20 plus feet. His left index finger shows where the cut ended, and upon close inspection the blade had a thinness of perhaps 1/8 of an inch, or 3 mm. As far as I know, no such saw blades of those dimensions exist today. The thinness is also apparent in the fact that rather than cutting in a perfectly flat line, the blade flexed, as one can see if you feel the surface, and was moving through this rather hard stone at about 3 mm, or 1/8 of an inch per revolution.

Detail view shows the path of the saw blade

Curious stone bowl in front of a water channel

Massive sculpted limestone blocks attributed to the Khemitians

There are a total of 14 pyramids at this site, which served as the main royal necropolis during the Fifth dynasty. The quality of construction of the Abusir pyramids is inferior to those presumed to have been of the Fourth Dynasty; perhaps signalling a decrease in royal power or a less vibrant economy. They are smaller than their predecessors, and are built of low quality local stone. Or, as I and others assert, the so called Forth Dynasty pyramids of Giza are far older than the other so called pyramids, made by a different culture; possibly the Khemitians. However, most Egyptologists clearly either disregard the presence of lost ancient high technology, or perhaps don't even see the many examples present at Abusir.

All of the major pyramids at Abusir were built as step pyramids, although the largest of them, the Pyramid of Neferirkare, is believed to have originally been built as a step pyramid some seventy metres in height and then later transformed into a "true" pyramid by having its steps filled in with loose masonry.

What is most intriguing for those interested in lost ancient technology are also the many core drill holes to be found at Abusir, especially in pink and black granite.

Two of many drill holes present at Abusir

Ney Sayers will of course dismiss the above photo as being either a modern fabrication or something that the dynastic Egyptians could have created with a copper tube with saw teeth cut into one end, some quartz sand, and water used as a lubricant. The many engineers that we have had on tour with us to this site and others that have evidence of core drilling dismiss such a crude technological approach immediately.

Close up showing tube drill grooves

And the above close up shows the actual feed or cutting rate of the tube drill as it ploughed into this black granite. Engineers and perhaps especially Chris Dunn who has spent more than 40 years working with drills and far more complex machines in the aviation and other industries find these holes intriguing.

And in even greater detail

Each revolution of the drill bit appears to have penetrated up to 2 mm, or more than 1/16 of an inch into the granite, which is astonishing, even when compared to what modern tools can do. Whatever this ancient technology was, it was able to cut into the stone more efficiently than what we have today, not necessarily faster, but removing more material per revolution.

Drill hole in rose granite

Craig, an electrician in the above photo was not only impressed by the hole he is looking at, but by the number of them at Abusir; the more we looked, the more we found.

More black granite drill holes

Yousef and the curious shaped slab

And then we were bewildered by what Yousef showed us next. Recent excavations at Abusir had unearthed this shaped stone that even the geologists who were with us could not positively identify as to rock type, though they did say it was very fine grained, hard and dense. The fact that it was cut with a saw of some kind will become painfully obvious in the following photos.

Obvious saw marks and termination of a cut

Like the large basalt slab that Yousef was looking at in a photo on a previous page, here we can see that a saw was at work, and then stopped short of finishing the cut on the left side of the block. The idea that this work was done with some kind of hand saw is as unlikely as that of the basalt block, because the feed rate is even and thus more typical of a powered machine than the work of human muscle.

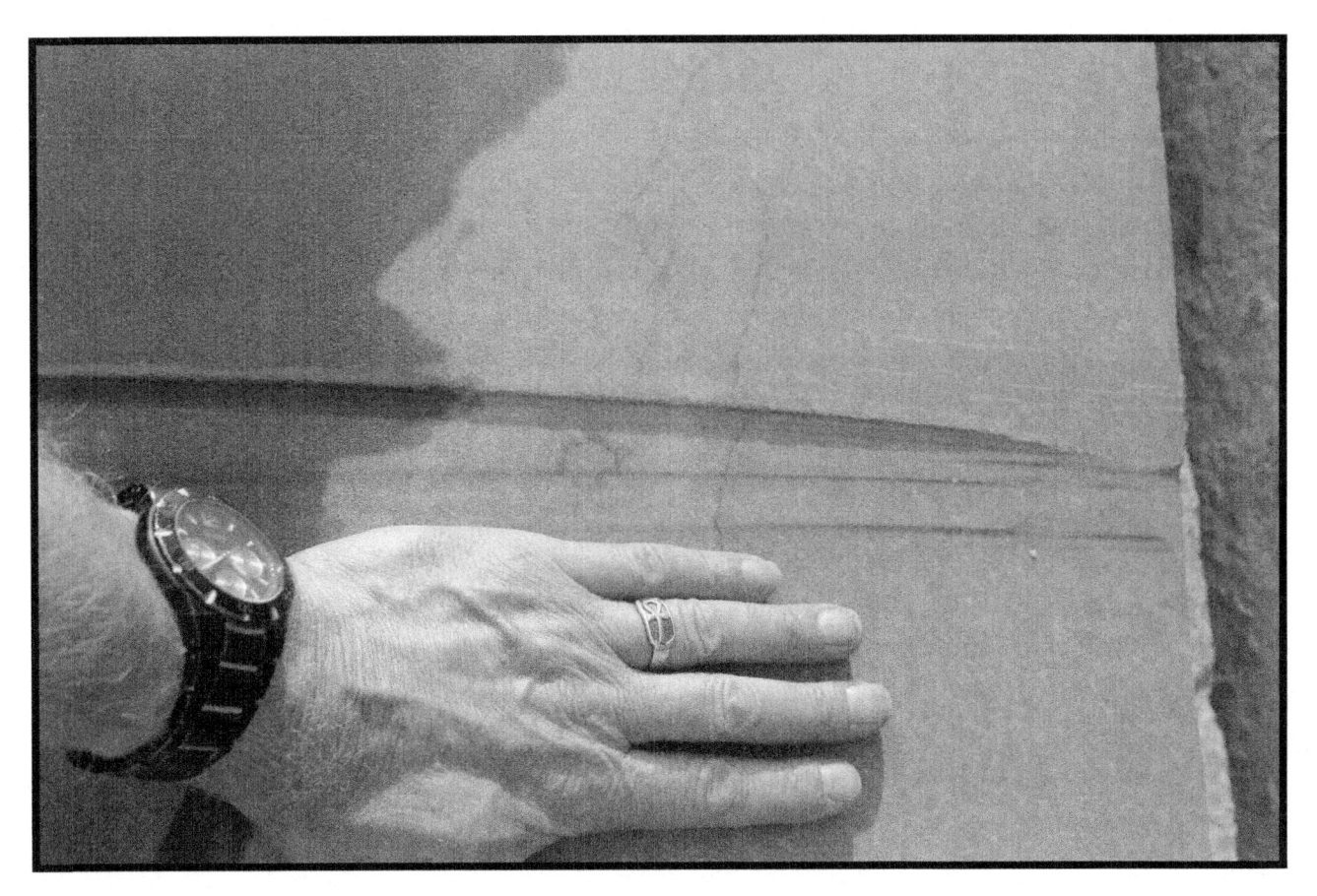

Evidence that the saw changed its cutting path

The saw appears to have clearly gone out of alignment and so the cutting pattern changed several times over the course of a few centimeters. This is typical, in modern times at least of a dull blade, or inattentive operator. Whether this was the case as regards the above stone is of course unknown, and the fact that it was unfinished and found buried may be evidence that it was cast aside as a flaw.

14/ Abugurab

Abugurab (also known as Abu Ghurab, Abu Gurob and Abu Jirab) is where a so called sun temple was found. It was excavated by Egyptologists between 1898 and 1901 led by Ludwig Borchardt on behalf of the Berlin Museum and is located just north of Abusir. The temple was supposedly constructed by the orders of Nyuserre Ini, the sixth king of the fifth dynasty of Egypt. The exact dates of his reign are unknown, but it is estimated that he came to the throne between 2450 BC and 2430 BC. He is also known for having been responsible for constructing a pyramid and burial chamber at Abu Sir.

I had the great opportunity in 2013 to visit Abugurab privately with Yousef Awyan, after we had explored Abusir. Rather than drive from Abusir to Abugurab, which is a reasonably short journey, we trekked across the sand. Along the way, about half way between the two sites we had to cross over a small mound, of which I did not pay much attention until I saw yet even more drill holes in some of the stones.

Rose granite with matching drill holes

Detail of one of the holes; hand showing scale

This photo shows the thinness of the drill core bit

The main temple at Abugurab was built on a natural hill that had been enhanced. Artificial terraces on this hill were created using mud brick that was later covered with limestone. And then the temple was built on top of these terraces. The temple is rectangular. The entrance is in the east side. Inside the temple is a large, open courtyard. At the western end of the courtyard are the ruins of a large stone obelisk, purported to be symbolizing the resting place of the Sun/Ra. The obelisk's base is a pedestal, with sloping sides and a square top. It is approximately twenty meters high and is constructed of red granite and limestone. Estimates of the combined height of the obelisk and base vary. Most likely, the total height was between fifty and seventy meters.

Approach to Abugurab from Abusir

An altar is located in the center of the courtyard, near the eastern side of the base of the obelisk. It was constructed from five large blocks of alabaster, which are arranged to form a symbol that can be translated, according to most Egyptologists as "May Ra be satisfied". What is astonishing about this "altar" is that it is mostly intact, whereas most other structures in the area have been ruthlessly damaged and quarried over the course of time. According to Stephen Mehler's account in *Land of Osiris*, ancient Khemitian oral tradition says Abugurab was already ancient by the time of the 5th Dynasty, and his teacher, Abd'El Hakim Awyan said the site was designed to create heightened spiritual awareness through the use of vibrations transmitted through the alabaster and other materials.

The massive alabaster hotep

From a builder's perspective, it is indeed amazing that the slabs of alabaster, which are so uniform in colour and composition that one would assume they all came from the same quarry. Of course it could be said that the reasoning behind this was for visual continuity, however, if one considers the vibrational aspect as believed by Abd'El Hakim Awyan, this too is a possible reason. Notice that the laying of the stone is horizontal in all of the sections; this was clearly intentional.

Greater detail of the hotep in this photo

From a lost ancient technology aspect, the circular center of the alabaster platform, as well as the smooth sides, even radius of the vertical and horizontal planes and especially circular indentations, presumably the work of a tube drill suggest advanced machining. The great four sided while alabaster altar was formed from four so called hotep signs oriented towards the cardinal directions and surrounding the great round circle described by some as a large solar disk. The hotep sign means "offering, "satisfied" or "peace", and is commonly found at the bottom of false doors in Old Kingdom tombs. The altar therefore actually says "Re is satisfied' in the four principal directions. The center element, a cylindrical block of alabaster, has a diameter of 1.8 m (6 ft.) (43)

Evidence of core drilling in the hotep

Sense of scale

More evidence of either core drill or router like machine

In the upper temple, the covered causeway opened up into a large open court flanked on the north by a row of annexes (storage magazines). There was also an area on the north for cattle to be slaughtered as offerings to the sun god. This slaughter area, when discovered, included limestone pavement that had been raised about 13 cm (6 in) above the level of the surrounding court. It had channels carved in the upper surface that probably drained down to a row of nine large alabaster basins about 1.18 m (3 ft, 8 in) in diameter. However, some Egyptologists like Miroslav Verner believe that this area was not for slaughter, because there were no tethering stones, flint knives or bones found; evidence that has been present at other sites where animals were slaughtered.

The curious alabaster bowls at Abugurab

Also, the bowls have strange knob like protrusions around the rim, each one with a different number of them and of no obvious purpose. And any bowl that would be used to hold liquid that could easily be drained and cleaned would have a hole in the center of the bottom, not half way up the side as seen as those found in the area. The astonishing roundness of each hole also suggests the use of a tube drill, and not some hand tool was at work to cut them out.

Detail photo showing the strange protrusions

The precision holes are readily apparent

Detail shot of one of the holes

Back towards the alabaster hotep assemblage, and in fact on the other side of it are other stone "bowls" made of limestone. They are relatively of the same size as those of alabaster, but rather than having one central hole on one side, they have three. It is unlikely that these and the other "bowls" were originally found where they are presently located, but were lined up by archaeologists for display, or eventual removal to a museum.

The other "bowls" found at Abugurab

Close up detail of the triple holes

15/ Giza Plateau

The Giza plateau area is of course the most famous archaeological site in Egypt, mainly because of the presence of the three large pyramids, known collectively as the "Great Pyramids" and the Sphinx. However, there are also a number of smaller pyramids in the area, as well as numerous tombs, ancient workers' villages and so on; an enormous site. It is located some 9 km (5 mi) inland into the desert from the old town of Giza on the Nile, and some 25 km (15 mi) southwest of Cairo city centre. The pyramids, which have historically loomed large as emblems of ancient Egypt in the Western imagination, (44) were popularized in Hellenistic times, when the Great Pyramid was listed by Antipater of Sidon as one of the Seven Wonders of the World. It is by far the oldest of the ancient Wonders and the only one still in existence. The question is, how old?

The grandeur of the Giza Plateau

The Pyramids of Giza consist of the Great Pyramid of Giza (known as the *Great Pyramid* and the *Pyramid of Cheops and Khufu*), the somewhat smaller Pyramid of

Khafre (or Chephren) a few hundred meters to the south west, and the relatively modest sized Pyramid of Menkaure (or Mykerinos) a few hundred meters further south west. The Great Sphinx lies on the east side of the complex. Along with these major monuments are a number of smaller satellite edifices, known as "queens" pyramids, causeways and valley pyramids.

The Giza Pyramids have been researched since the dawn of modern history. Piles of books have been written about the enigmatic Great Pyramid alone, and many of these books stem from Egyptian and foreign archaeologists. These Egyptologists, in general haven't changed their view about the Great Pyramid very much in the last hundred years, dating the construction back to 2589 B.C. supposedly created as a burial site, the tomb of pharaoh Khufu (Cheops in Greek). One of the leading pyramid experts is Dr. Zahi Hawass, the now ex-chairman of the Supreme Council of Antiquities (SCA) in Egypt, who fiercely adheres to the tomb theory of the Great Pyramid. Although there is a so called sarcophagus inside the King's chamber of the Great Pyramid, no mummy has ever been found inside this pyramid, or the other two large ones at Giza. This "sarcophagus" must have been made inside the pyramid since due to its size it cannot be removed from the King's chamber any more.

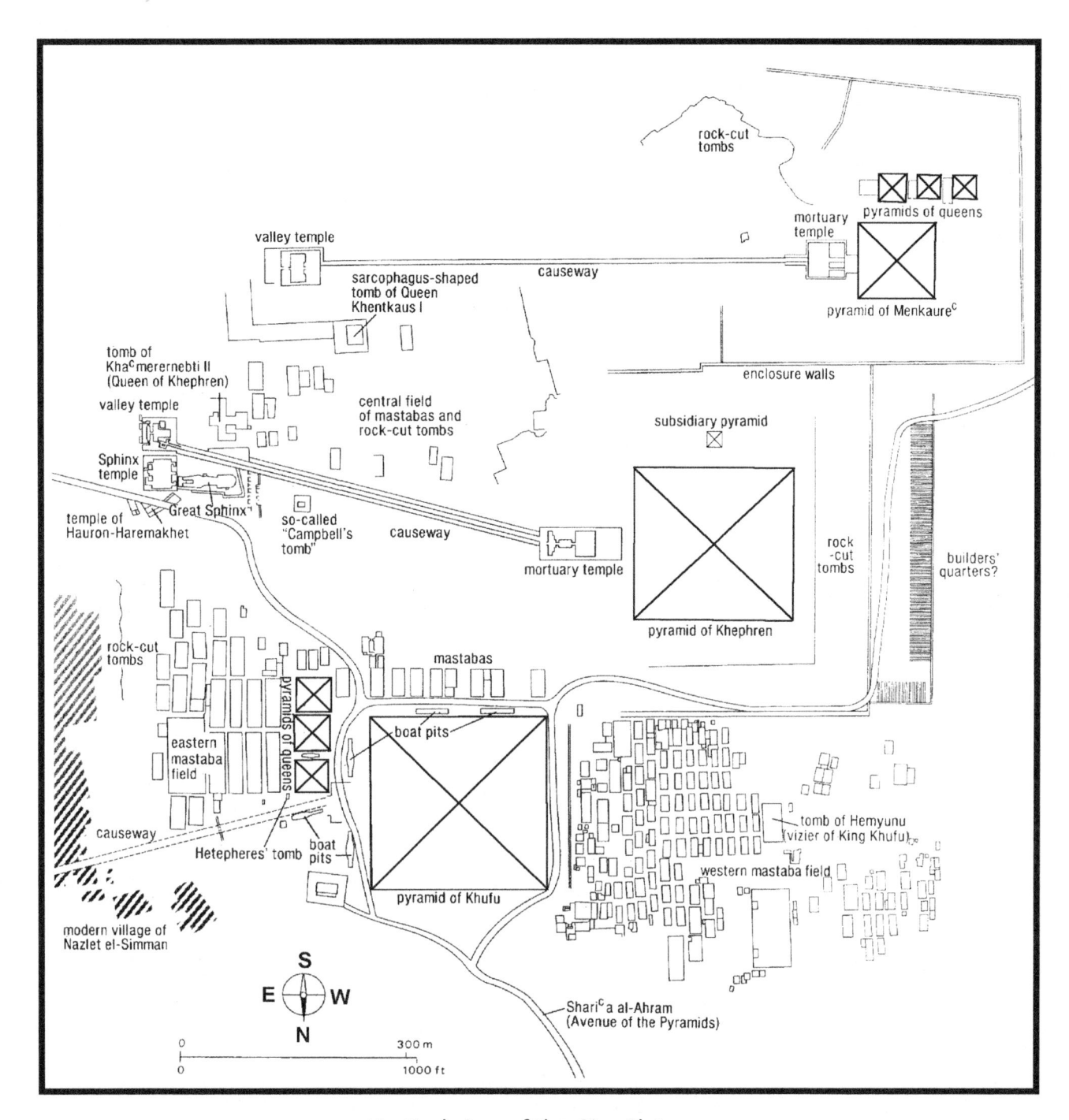

Vertical view of the Giza Plateau

In the last decade scientists have started to doubt the age and purpose of the Great Pyramids. Gradually as they reveal more of their secrets, the tomb theory becomes less acceptable. Indications are that the Great Pyramids must have been built by a highly intelligent and technological civilization that must have had a scientific understanding and access to techniques that may have even beyond our own.

The Great Pyramid of "Khufu" for example consists of some 2,300,000 limestone blocks, has the height of a forty story building and the width of two and a half football fields, having an overall footprint of 13 acres. The foundation of the pyramid is chiseled into the bedrock with a precision of only 2 centimetres (less than one inch) off perfect level. Even today with all our technical knowhow and laser precision craftsmanship according to specialists we would be very hard pressed to be able to build a structure like the Great Pyramid which such precision.

In fact attempts have been made to prove that the pyramid could be constructed using the known ancient Egyptian tools and methods. Egyptologist Mark Lehner has made an attempt with a large group of people but failed to even create a 6 m scale model of the pyramid. He had to call in the help of a truck with a winch to get the blocks out of the quarry. In the late seventies a Japanese team funded by Nissan made another attempt to create an 18 m high scale model using the same primitive ancient Egyptian tools such as chisels and hammers. The once so proud Japanese team returned home disillusioned and embarrassed, since they had to use jackhammers to cut the hard stone, were unable to get the stones across the Nile and eventually had to use bulldozers, a truck and even a helicopter to get the blocks stacked to a pile that remotely resembled a pyramid. In both attempts made to reconstruct the pyramid, only small blocks were carved from the quarry but remember that the real pyramid contains blocks had the weight of a steam engine locomotive. (46)

Egyptologists' opinion of how the pyramids were made

Also consider that these stones are so precisely carved and the mortar joints so terribly thin that you can't even get a sheet of paper in between them in many cases. The mortar joints are very strong, far stronger that the mortar that we use nowadays, such that the stones seem more or less glued or fused together. The smallest blocks weigh a ton, while the average block however weighs 2.5 tons up to even 70 tons. How could the Egyptians lift these very heavy blocks with such precision to the height of a forty-story building? Although there are some theories, we simply don't know for sure. The massive construction of the pyramid is also aligned with a precision of only 3 minutes and 6 seconds off perfect alignment to the 4 cardinal points.

Clear evidence of ancient quarrying on the Giza Plateau

The photo above shows clearly that next to the second pyramid (on the right) there is a quarry. Since the shape and size of the residual rectangles on the ground correspond with the size of many of the stones that make up the core of the pyramid, it is quite reasonable to assume that this is in fact the quarry for the second pyramid, as well as perhaps for the others on the Giza Plateau. And the wall on the left shows the original height of the plateau, as well as how far down the stone cutting occurred.

The sarcophagi that were found inside the chambers of the pyramids are made of extremely hard granite, most likely from Aswan. Although no mummy was ever found inside these sarcophagi, Egyptologists still want us to believe that they were used as coffins. They even came up with the primitive tools that were used to hollow the granite blocks for the sarcophagus; a hard dolorite ball on a stick used to batter the rock, copper and bronze chisels, and sand used as a levelling and finishing compound.

In 1995, Christopher Dunn investigated the sarcophagus of the Khafre pyramid. He had brought along with him some precision instruments and climbed inside the sarcophagus to measure the smoothness of the interior in order to determine the degree of precision that had been used in the shaping of the box. What he found was nothing less than astonishing; the inside of the box was so perfectly smooth and flat, that a flashlight shone from behind a straight edge would not reveal any light passing through. All edges in the box were perfectly square and the surfaces almost perfectly flat. The curvature of the inside corners was so small and the edges so sharp, that it is totally impossible that these corners were created by battering with balls with the diameter they are supposed to have. Since Dunn couldn't measure a single deviation from a somewhat perfectly flat surfaces and perfect square corners, in his enthusiasm and utter amazement from his discovery he yelled 'Space-Age precision'.

It has become more and more obvious that the Great Pyramid in particular and the Giza Plateau in general has been designed to encode sophisticated scientific knowledge in many ways, there seem to be no coincidences. Every discovered detail has a meaning than we've just started to unravel. For centuries the Giza plateau has been studied through the eyes of archaeologists and historians but in the last two decades that has changed.

The sheer grandeur of the Great Pyramid

Originally the Great Pyramid was covered with a 144,000 white tura limestone casing stones, giving it a smooth polished surface. The tura stone is not found on the Giza plateau, where most of the blocks to create the pyramids were quarried. Tura limestone was found deep underground about half way between modern day Cairo and the city of Helwan, and instead of open pit mining, the miners tunnelled deep to cut large stones out, leaving some limestone behind to support the caverns left behind. In ancient times the reflections from the Sun must have been noticeable from miles away. The Egyptians called their pyramid 'Ta Khut' which translates into 'The Light'. Muslims and other cultures in later times may have robbed the Great Pyramid of its casing stones to build the mosques in Cairo. The only remains of the casing stones are found at the base of the Great Pyramid and the top of the pyramid of Khafre. It is from these stones that the exact dimensions of the Pyramids have been determined. The capstone that should seal the top of the Great Pyramid is missing, if it in fact ever existed.

What is left of the casing stones on the Great Pyramid

The tightness of the fit is almost surreal

Joseph Davidovits (born 1935) is a French materials scientist known for the invention of geopolymer chemistry. He posited that the blocks of the Great Pyramid are not carved stone but mostly a form of limestone concrete. Davidovits was not convinced that the ancient Egyptians possessed the tools or technology to carve and haul the huge (2.5 to 15 ton) limestone blocks that made up the Great Pyramid. Davidovits suggested that the blocks were molded in place by using a form of limestone concrete. According to his theory, a soft limestone with high kaolinite content was quarried in the wadi on the south of the Giza plateau. It was then dissolved in large, Nile fed pools until it became watery slurry. Lime (found in the ash of ancient cooking fires) and natron (also used by the Egyptians in mummification) was mixed in. The pools were then left to evaporate, leaving behind a moist, clay-like mixture. This wet "concrete" would be carried to the construction site where it would be packed into reusable wooden molds. In the next few days the mixture would undergo a chemical hydration reaction similar to the setting of cement.

Using Davidovits' theory, no large gangs would be needed to haul blocks and no huge and unwieldy ramps would be needed to transport the blocks up the side of the pyramid. Also, no chiseling or carving with soft bronze tools would be required to dress their surfaces and new blocks could be cast in place, on top of and pressed against the old blocks. This would account for the unerring precision of the joints of the casing stones (the blocks of the core show tools marks and were cut with much lower tolerances). Proof of concept experiments using similar compounds were carried out at Davidovits' geopolymer institute in northern France. It was found that a crew of ten, working with simple hand tools, could build a structure of fourteen, 1.3 to 4.5 ton blocks in a couple of days. According to Davidovits the architects possessed at least two concrete formulas: one for the large structural blocks and another for the white casing stones. He argues earlier pyramids, brick structures, and stone vases were built using similar techniques.

Although his ideas are not accepted by mainstream Egyptologists or many other researchers, in December 2006 Michel Barsoum, Adrish Ganguly, and Gilles Hug published a peer reviewed paper in the *Journal of the American Ceramic Society* stating that parts of the pyramid were cast with a type of limestone concrete. (47) However, Dipayan Jana, a petrographer, made a presentation to the ICMA (International Cement Microscopy Association) in 2007 and gave a paper in which he concludes "we are far from accepting even as a remote possibility of a 'man made' origin of pyramid stones." (48) And this has been echoed in personal discussions with author Stephen Mehler, geologist Robert Schoch and others.

Mehler has submitted several limestone samples from the Great Pyramid to Dr. George Bayer, senior scientist at Matco Associates, a materials testing lab in Pittsburgh, P.A. Dr. Bayer found no evidence in any of the samples, be them from the casing stone, or the core.

To simply call this mortar free is an understatement

In *The Great Pyramid Decoded*, Peter Lemesurier writes, "It would be a rash man who undertook to find, even today, a building more accurately aligned to the True cardinal points of the compass, masonry more finely jointed, or facing-stones more immaculately dressed.... the sceptic may doubt that many of the pyramid's stones -- some of them weighing up to seventy tons -- were so finely cut and positioned as to give joints of less than a fiftieth of an inch in thickness; ...he may scoff at the claim that a fine cement was run into these joints so expertly as to give an even coverage of single areas as big as five feet by seven *in the vertical*; he may express profound disbelief when it is pointed out to him that the building's now almost totally despoiled original outer casing of polished limestone (all twenty-one acres of it) was levelled and honed to the standard of accuracy normal in modern optical work. But these, as it happens, are facts which anybody may check who cares to."

As stated earlier, the casing stones of the Great Pyramid, so called Khufu were of pure Tura limestone. In AD 1300, a massive earthquake loosened many of the outer casing stones, which were then carted away by Bahri Sultan An-Nasir Nasir-ad-Din al-Hasan in 1356 to build mosques and fortresses in nearby Cairo. Many more casing stones were removed from the great pyramids by Muhammed Ali Pasha in the early 19th century to build the upper portion of his Alabaster Mosque in Cairo not far from Giza. These limestone casings can still be seen as parts of these structures. Later explorers reported massive piles of rubble at the base of the pyramids left over from the continuing collapse of the casing stones, which were subsequently cleared away during continuing excavations of the site. Nevertheless, a few of the casing stones from the lowest course can be seen to this day *in situ* around the base of the Great Pyramid, and display the same workmanship and precision that has been reported for centuries. Petrie also found a different orientation in the core and in the casing measuring 193 centimetres ± 25 centimetres. He suggested a re-determination of north was made after the construction of the core, but a mistake was made, and the casing was built with a different orientation. Petrie related the precision of the casing stones as to being "equal to opticians' work of the present day, but on a scale of acres" and "to place such stones in exact contact would be careful work; but to do so with cement in the joints seems almost impossible". (49)

The majority of the casing stones of the second or Khafre pyramid were also tura limestone, with lowest row being red granite, most likely from Aswan. And the third or Menkaure pyramid as well was mainly tura limestone as regards casing stones, with the lowest 16 layers being red granite. (50) But why would that be? Surely not for aesthetic reasons one would presume, and it would take far more effort to bring the granite from Aswan, some 500 miles away, than the far more local tura quarry.

Casing stones on the Menkaure Pyramid with protrusions

Detail view of the rose granite casing stones

Another peculiarity about the granite casing stones of the Menkaure pyramid is that many of them have obvious protrusions, what some might call knobs. Since what is left of the cased areas show very tight joints, it can hardly be said that the wall was somehow left unfinished. Very similar knobs are found on ancient walls in Cusco Peru, said to have been made by the Inca culture (which is questionable.) The standard academic reasoning as to why these knobs are on the Cusco walls is that they were intentionally left there to assist in the lifting of the stones into position. However, when asked why some of the larger stones do not have these protrusions, the answer is that they had already been cut off, and the builders never got around to finishing the job.

Green andesite wall in Cusco Peru

A further curious point about the Great Pyramid is that it has in fact 8 sides, and not 4. One very unusual feature of the Great Pyramid is a concavity of the core that makes the monument an eight-sided figure, rather than four-sided like every other Egyptian pyramid. That is to say, that its four sides are hollowed in or indented along their central lines, from base to peak. This concavity divides each of the apparent four sides in half, creating a very special and unusual eight-sided pyramid; and it is executed to such an extraordinary degree of precision as to enter the realm of the uncanny. For, viewed from any ground position or distance, this concavity is quite invisible to the naked eye. The hollowing-in can be noticed only from the air, and only at certain times of the day, (51) and usually days of the year when the sun is at the right angle in association with the pyramid.

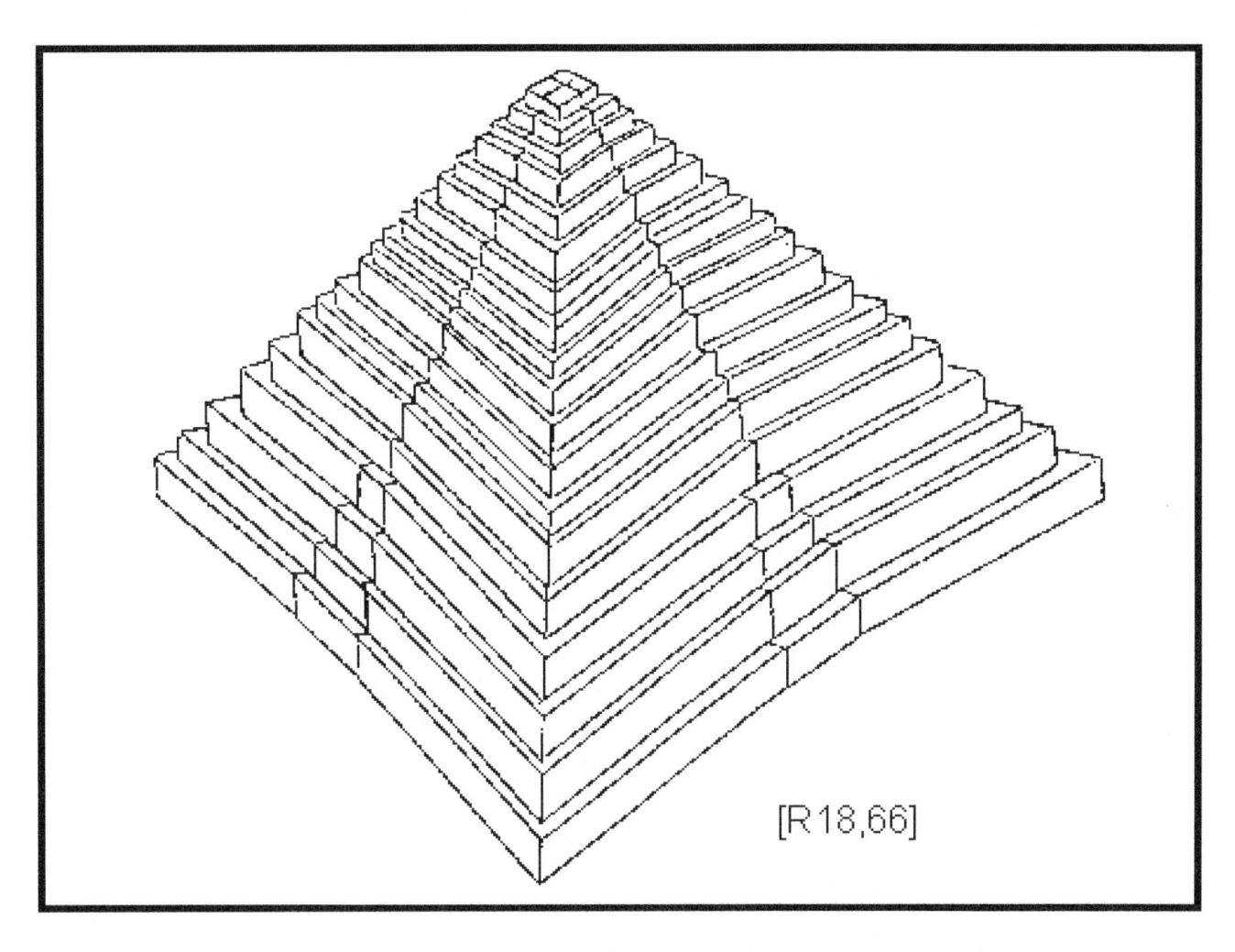

Exaggerated view of the 8 sided pyramid

It was discovered quite by accident in 1940, when a British Air Force pilot, P. Groves, was flying over the pyramid. This strange feature was not first observed in 1940. It was illustrated in La Description de l'Egypte in the late 1700's (Volume V, pl. 8). Flinders Petrie noticed a hollowing in the core masonry in the center of each face and wrote that he "continually observed that the courses of the core had dips of as much as ½° to 1°." (52) The question of course is why would these indentations be there, and were they on purpose. Maragioglio and Rinaldi felt this feature would help bond the casing to the core. Verner agreed: "As in the case of the earlier Red Pyramid, the slightly concave walls were intended to increase the stability of the pyramid's mantle, i.e. casing stones. (53)

Martin Isler outlined the various theories in his article "Concerning the Concave Faces on the Great Pyramid": (54)

1/ to give a curved form to the nucleus in order to prevent the faces from sliding.

2/ the casing block in the center would be larger and would serve more suitably as a guide for other blocks in the same course.

3/ to better bond the nucleus to the casing.

4/ for aesthetic reasons, as concave faces would make the structure more pleasing to the eye.

5/ when the casing stones were later removed; they were tumbled down the faces, and thereby wore down the center of the pyramids more than the edges.

6/ natural erosion of wind-swept sand had a greater effect on the center.

Isler dismisses the first four reasons based on the idea that "what is proposed for the first pyramid should hold true for the others." He also dismisses the last two because they would not "dip the courses," but rather have simply "worn away the surface of the stone." Adding another category to the list above, "a result of imperfect building method," he proceeds to theorize that the concavity was an artifact of a compounding error in building technique (specifically, a sag in the mason's line). One is tempted to reject this theory based on Isler's own reasoning: "what is proposed for the first pyramid should hold true for the others." Also, the fact that the "sag" appears even on all four sides would mean that the builders would have to have repeated their mistake on such a grand scale.

Other clues as to the complexity of the exterior of the Great Pyramids can be seen if you look at the exposed limestone bedrock and what is left of some of the flooring. Most visitors are not shown these features, as many of the tour guides are frankly not even aware of them, but if you have a guide like Yousef Awyan, the evidence is quite clear.

The sculpted bedrock of the Giza Plateau

The photo above shows the actual limestone bedrock on which the Great Pyramids sit. The recessed areas show that both the external basalt flooring on one side of the Great Pyramid was integrated into the bedrock in a three dimensional manner, as was the pyramid itself.

Obvious evidence of saws cutting through basalt

The basalt flooring was heavily looted over the course of time, but the exposed sides, such as the photo above shows clear evidence of a saw at work. Taking into account that basalt is 8 on the Mohs scale, bronze tools, or even iron ones could not have made these cuts. But it gets even more curious when we look at the following 2 photographs.

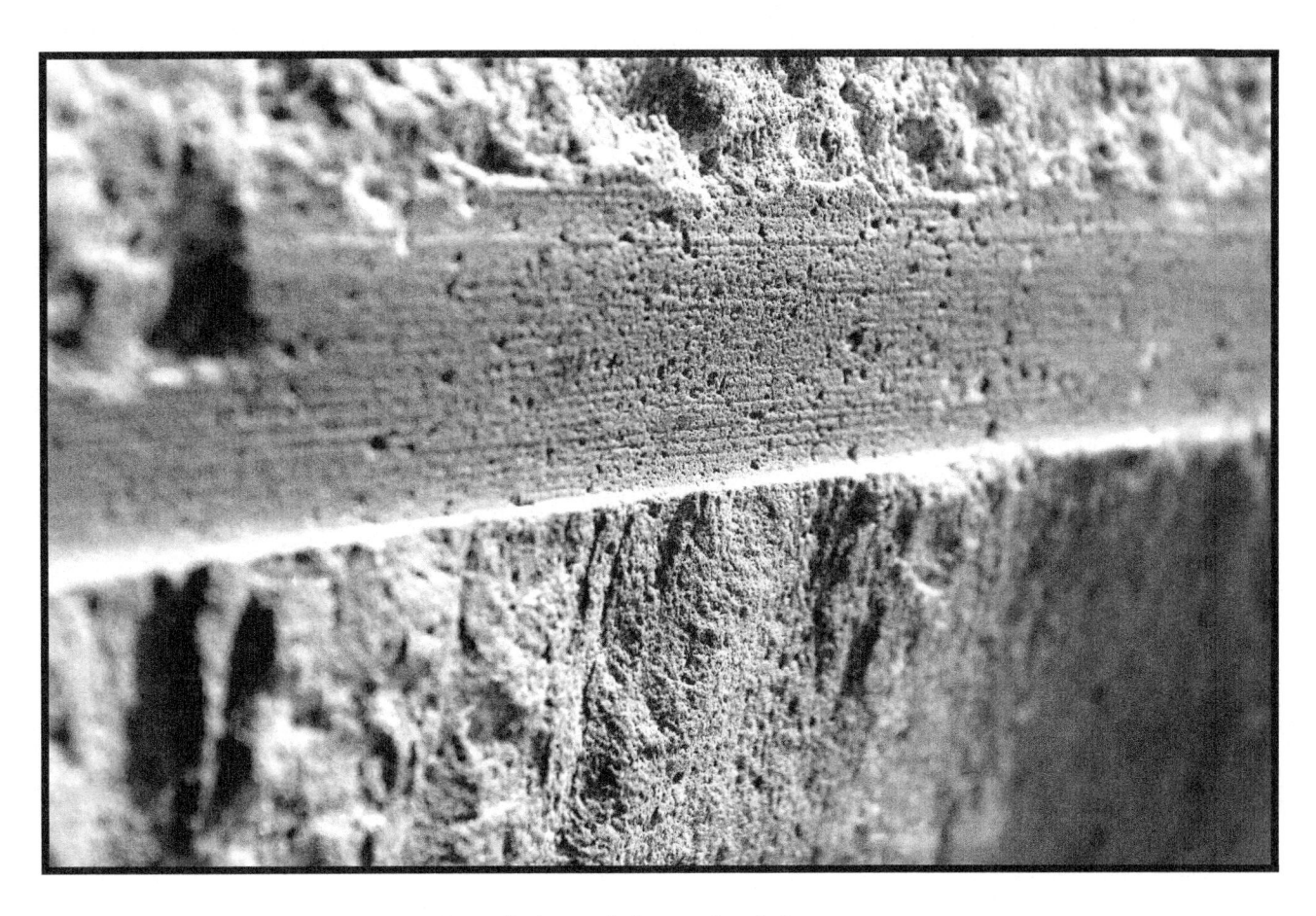

Detail view of the path of the saw

The saw was cutting at least 2 mm per revolution

What you see in the horizontal lines are the actual saw marks. Like with the basalt examples at Abusir, the lines are even and evenly spaced at 2 mm per cut of the blade. Such smooth penetration of the stone tells us that the saw was not human driven, which would be more erratic due to the muscle powered work, so it must have been mechanized in some way. Also, the actual cutting material would need to be harder than basalt, and the only candidates that we know which can do this are tungsten carbide, corundum, silicon carbide and diamond.

Now that we have had a cursory look at the exterior of the three main Giza pyramids, it is now time to explore the interior. Though the second and third pyramids have internal passages and rooms, those of the Great Pyramid are the most complex, and shall be discussed here. The original entrance to the Great Pyramid is 17 m (56 ft) vertically above ground level and 7.29 m (23.9 ft) east of the center line of the pyramid. From this original entrance there is a Descending Passage 0.96 m (3.1 ft) high and 1.04 m (3.4 ft) wide which goes down at an angle of 26° 31'23" through the masonry of the pyramid and then into the limestone bedrock beneath it. After 105.23 m (345.2 ft), the passage becomes level and continues for an additional 8.84 m (29.0 ft) to the lower Chamber, which appears not to have been finished, according to most Egyptologists. There is a continuation of the horizontal passage in the south wall of the lower chamber and also a pit dug in the floor. Some Egyptologists suggest this Lower Chamber was intended to be the original burial chamber, but that Pharaoh Khufu later changed his mind and wanted it to be higher up in the pyramid. (55)

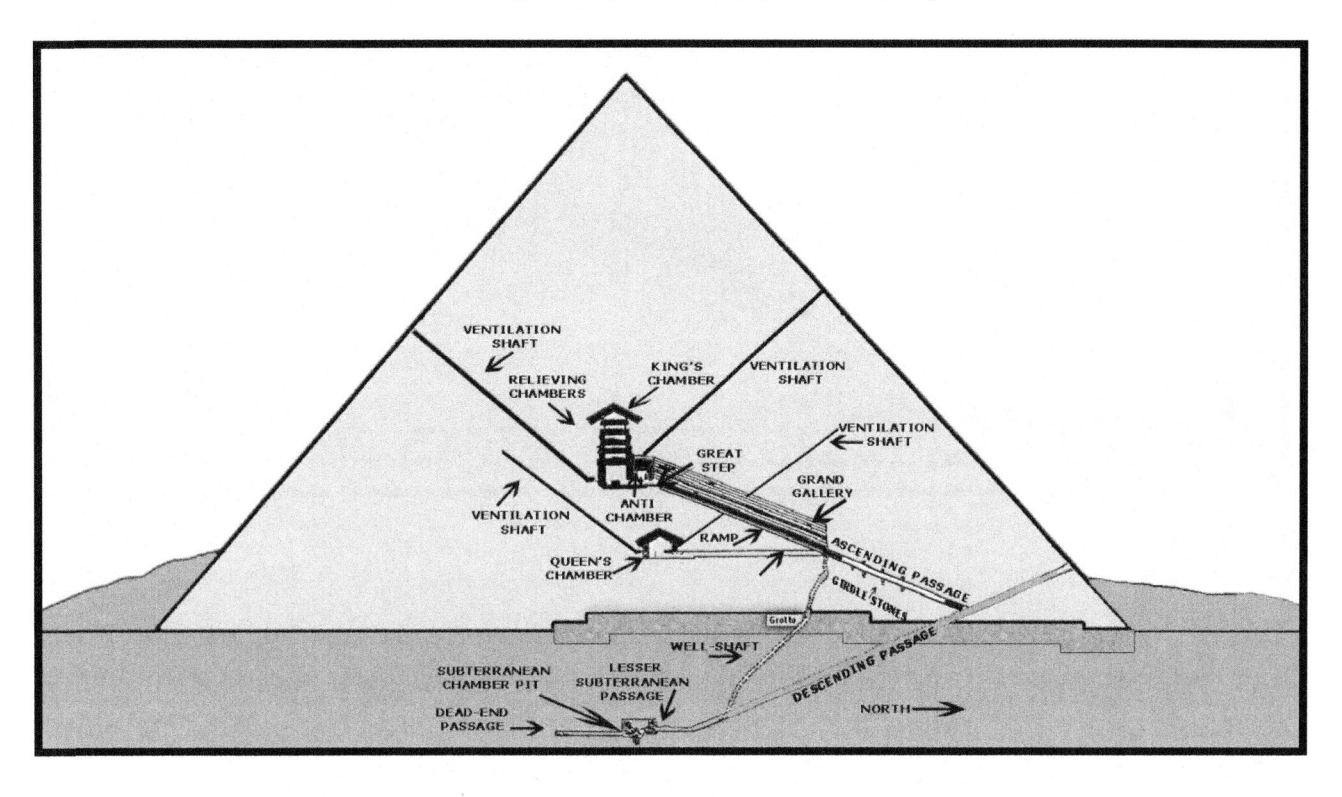

Basic cross section of the Great Pyramid

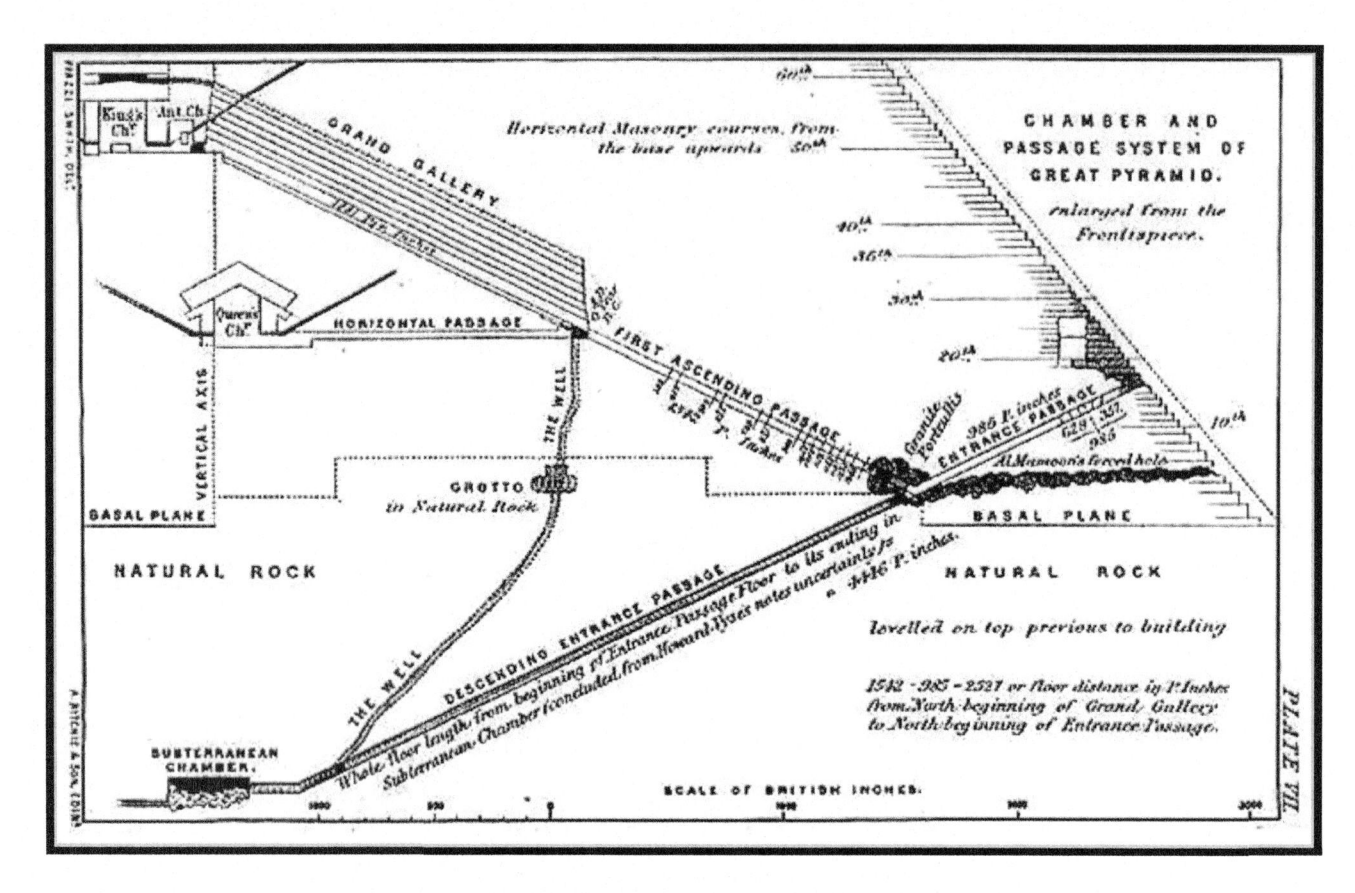

More detail of the interior of the Great Pyramid

The western half of the chamber has been carved nearly six feet higher than the eastern half and sculpted into several large fin-like protrusions. All these fin like protrusions are situated east to west and are nearly as tall as the ceiling. Between the large protrusions, a stepped channel starts at the floor and flows toward the back of the chamber. In its centre there is a channel leading to the western wall. In the southeastern corner, a tunnel known as the "dead end shaft," thirty inches in height and width, runs south fifty-seven feet, then ends at a wall. There are two other features in the design of the Great Pyramid that appear to be part of the work performed in the bedrock, the well shaft and the "grotto."

If the subterranean chamber was nothing more than a mistake, and was originally designed to be a burial vault, an enormous amount of resources was wasted. One could imagine, as most Egyptologists obviously do, that the fins and other surfaces above the floor was merely symbolic of a room being quarried as a tomb, and then stopped at the request of the fickle pharaoh. On the other hand, if the chamber was an integral part of the overall design of the Great Pyramid and performed a function, then what could that function possibly be? Everything from a tomb to temple of initiation to a device of some kind, there's never been a lack of theories over the years describing what the Great Pyramid of Giza and the other pyramids were originally designed for, and by whom.

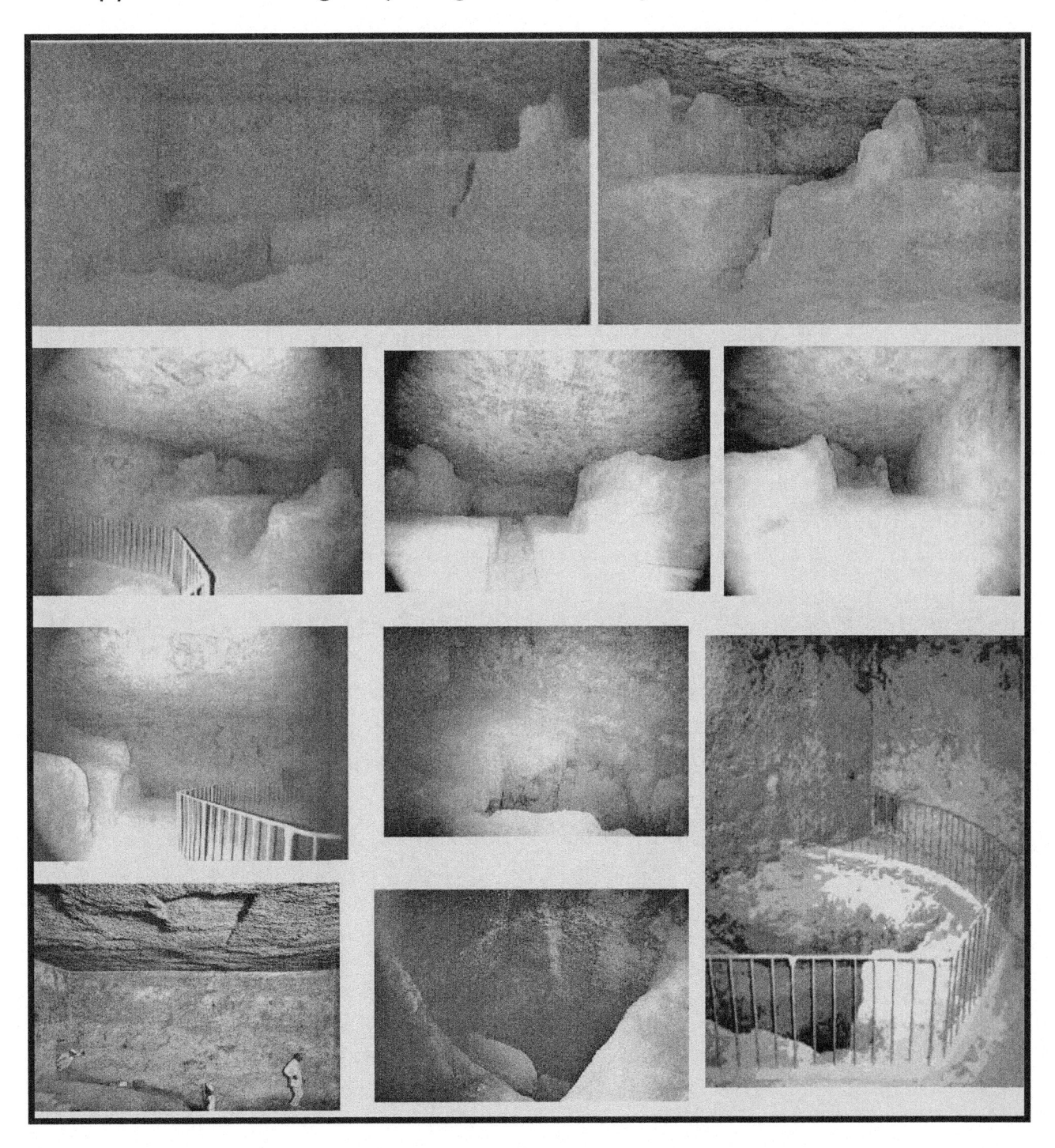

Photos of the subterranean chamber

In 1962, in a book entitled *The Pharaoh's Pump*, a man named Edward Kunkel put forward the theory that the Great Pyramid was in its entirety a water pump. Engineer John Cadman ran across the book one day browsing titles in a used bookstore. Intrigued, he purchased Kunkel's book and after reading it realized that Kunkel was not far off the mark with his water pump theory. Being familiar with hydraulics and machines that rely on hydraulics, Cadman noticed that the design of the Great Pyramid's subterranean chamber and its associated tunnels looked familiar.

Before the invention of the electric water pump the ram pump was used to move water from a reservoir to another location through a simple system that had only two moving parts, a weight loaded waste valve and check valve. Under the force of gravity, water in a reservoir flows down the input pipe and forces the waste value closed. With the waste valve closed, water continues to flow down the input pipe increasing the pressure inside the pump. The increased pressure opens the delivery valve forcing water into the output pipe. Since the water is being forced to a higher elevation faster than the water flowing down the input pipe the flow of water reverses which closes the check valve and the process begins again. (56)

Inspired by Kunkel's work, Cadman learned as much as he could about the Great Pyramid's subterranean chamber and associated tunnels, and in June of 1999 he made his first model. It leaked then cracked, neither would it function. Several months later he began work on a second model and connected a new line to the bottom of the pit shaft, believing this new line had to be the pressurized output. But the pump still didn't operate the way he thought it should so he began building a third model which he completed on April 3, 2000, and it worked flawlessly.

One of John Cadman's models

What Cadman discovered was that the subterranean chamber absorbed much of the reverse pulse. He also observed that without the subterranean chamber, the reverse pulse was large and the output flow was more erratic, confirming for him that the output in the Great Pyramid's subterranean chamber travelled through what is called the dead end shaft. It also confirmed his suspicion that the ancient oral tradition that a tunnel exists connecting the subterranean chamber's pit to the Nile River.

A few weeks later Cadman moved the model to a seasonal creek with a pond serving as a reservoir, and experimented further. To simulate the effect of being underground he encased the pump assembly in concrete (see figures 4 and 5). Interestingly, the action of the pump, which was now embedded in concrete, created a vertical compression wave. This, according to Cadman, meant that the Great Pyramid's subterranean ram pump also had an acoustical element. So, he built two more models to study the acoustics and fluid dynamics. The acoustic model, which was made of fibreglass and epoxy and encased in concrete, weighed five hundred pounds. When operating, the characteristic heartbeat-like thump of the pump could be felt through the ground twenty feet away and heard nearly a hundred feet away. Because of the powerful pulses it generated, Cadman named it the "pulse generator." (57)

Cadman's modelling of the subterranean chamber and its tunnels provides a better understanding of the Great Pyramid, as well as the Giza Plateau in general. In its completed state the Great Pyramid would have required a moat, which was fed by a system of aqueducts from the now extinct Western Nile (the Ur Nile); an ideal source for a gravity fed water system, since the Western Nile was at a higher elevation than the plateau. It also explains the remains of a retaining wall that once surrounded the pyramid. The wall served as an embankment for an onsite reservoir. Tunnels, such as the "well" at the pyramid's entrance, connected the Great Pyramid complex to an ancient lake, Lake Moeris, and the Western Nile.

Energy path in the subterranean chamber according to John Cadman

Lake Moeris was an ancient lake fifty miles southwest of Cairo. At one time it was very large and occupied the entire Faiyum depression. It was also called the Pure Lake and the Lake of Osiris by the ancient Egyptians. During prehistoric times the waters of Lake Moeris stood nearly 120 feet above sea level, but by 10,000 BC they had dropped to nearly twenty-five feet below sea level, possibly as a result of the Nile channel being naturally diverted. With increases from rain, between 9000 BCE and 4000 BC the lake rose again, but gradually subsided. And as the climate became increasingly more arid, a canal connected Lake Moeris to the Nile; over the years it slowly silted. During the Middle Kingdom, 2000 BCE to 1600 BC, dynastic Egyptians widened and deepened the channel, thereby restoring its flow. At that time the lake was believed to be fifty-five feet above sea level. So, if the lake was at its highest level prior to 10,000 BC, could this give us an indication of when the pump would have worked most efficiently, and thus help us to date the age of the Great Pyramid?

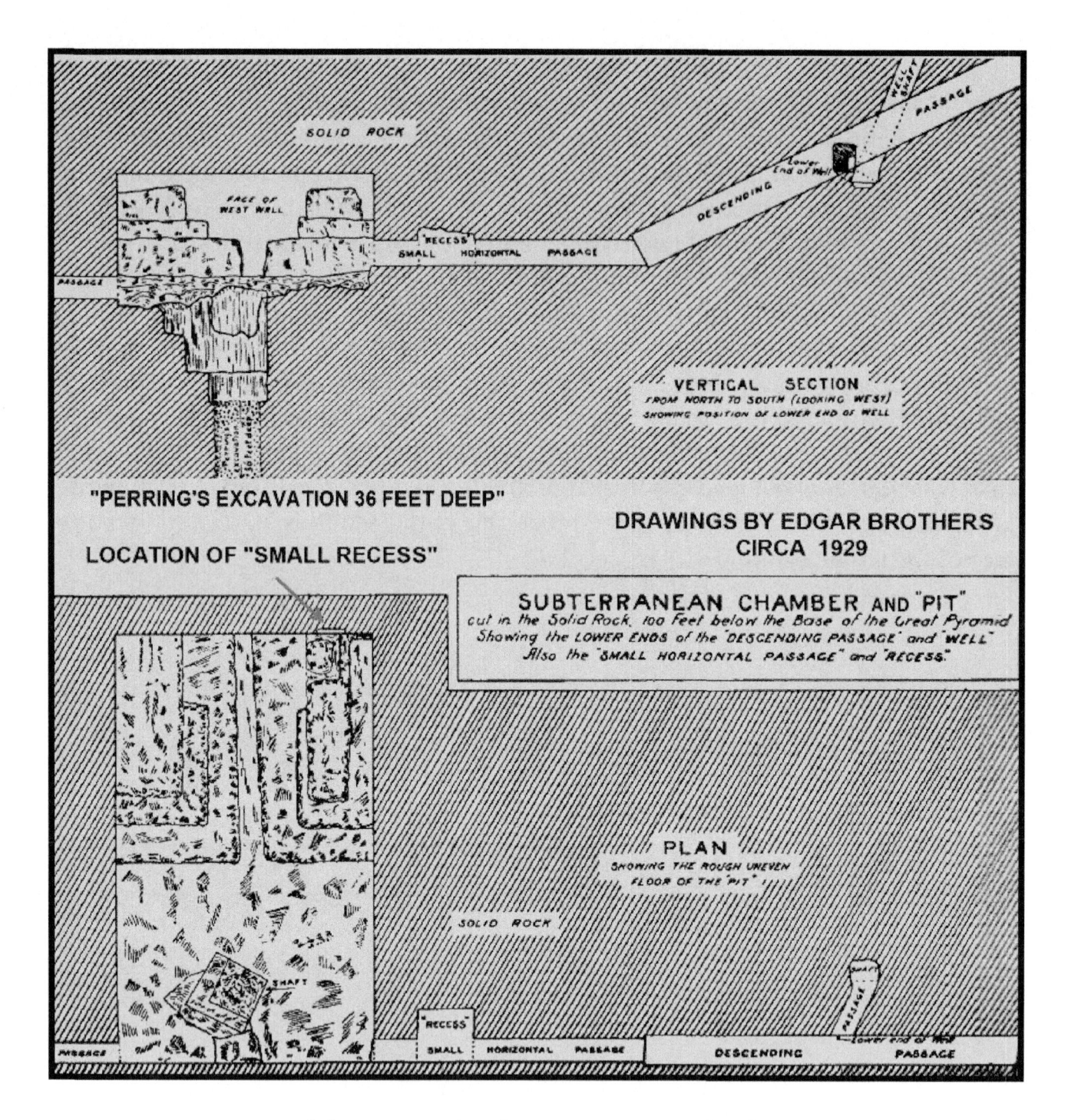

Subterranean chamber in even greater detail

If the Great Pyramid was just a water pump as John Cadman demonstrated in his experiments, then there wouldn't be a need for another chamber located in the middle of the pyramid (so called Queens') and a third chamber located in its upper regions (what is commonly called the King's chamber.) These chambers as well as the shafts in these two chambers need to be explained. Assuming Cadman is correct that the compression wave was what the pump was designed for, and then the middle and upper chamber would likely have been designed to somehow react with the vibrations emanating from the pump. The upper chamber in its entirety was built from slabs of granite as in the floor, walls, and ceiling, and located just above the chamber the builders of the Great Pyramid placed five rows of granite beams. So, it is obvious that granite was of primary importance in the uppermost chamber. The question is why. Clearly not for the aesthetic whim of a pharaoh, who did not even bother to carve inscriptions about himself anywhere inside the pyramid.

The Queen's Chamber is exactly half-way between the north and south faces of the pyramid and measures 5.75 m (18.9 ft) north to south, 5.23 m (17.2 ft) east to west, and has a pointed roof with an apex 6.23 m (20.4 ft) above the floor. At the eastern end of the chamber there is a niche 4.67 m (15.3 ft) high. The original depth of the niche was 1.04 m (3.4 ft), but has since been deepened by treasure hunters. In the north and south walls of the Queen's Chamber there are shafts, which unlike those in the King's Chamber that immediately slope upwards, are horizontal for around 2 m (6.6 ft) before sloping upwards. The horizontal distance was cut in 1872 by a British engineer, Waynman Dixon, who believed a similar shaft to the King's Chamber must also exist. He was proved right, but because the shafts are not connected to the outer faces of the pyramid or the Queen's Chamber, their purpose is unknown.

The so called Queens Chamber received its name from Arab explorers, but even conventional scholars now agree that it was not actually intended to be the burial chamber of a queen. The chamber itself is made entirely of beautifully finished limestone blocks with a gabled ceiling. It sits on the twenty fifth course of masonry on the pyramids east west axis. The walls are bare of painted or inscribed hieroglyphics, but there is a niche in the east wall about four and a half meters up from the floor. The niche also has a corbel ceiling. It is possible that a statue of the king or his ka (soul) might have stood in the niche, but this is pure speculation. Mark Lehner argues that the Queen's Chamber would have been sealed off, transforming it into a Serdab (a room for the king´s spiritual soul or Ka) but that too is pure speculation.

Interior of the Queens Chamber

If not a tomb or depository of sculpture of the spiritual essence of a pharaoh, then what could be another reason why the so called Queen's Chamber exists? According to Chris Dunn, two chemicals, hydrated zinc chloride and dilute hydrochloric acid were mixed together to create hydrogen gas. But where did these chemicals come from? Dunn argues that they were pumped from an underground chamber up a vertical shaft and then fed by gravity through the so called "airshafts" which exit in the north and south walls of the Queen's Chamber. Moreover, he surmises that the flow of chemicals was triggered via copper cables which were attached to the back of the copper "handles" in the so called "Gantenbrink's door."

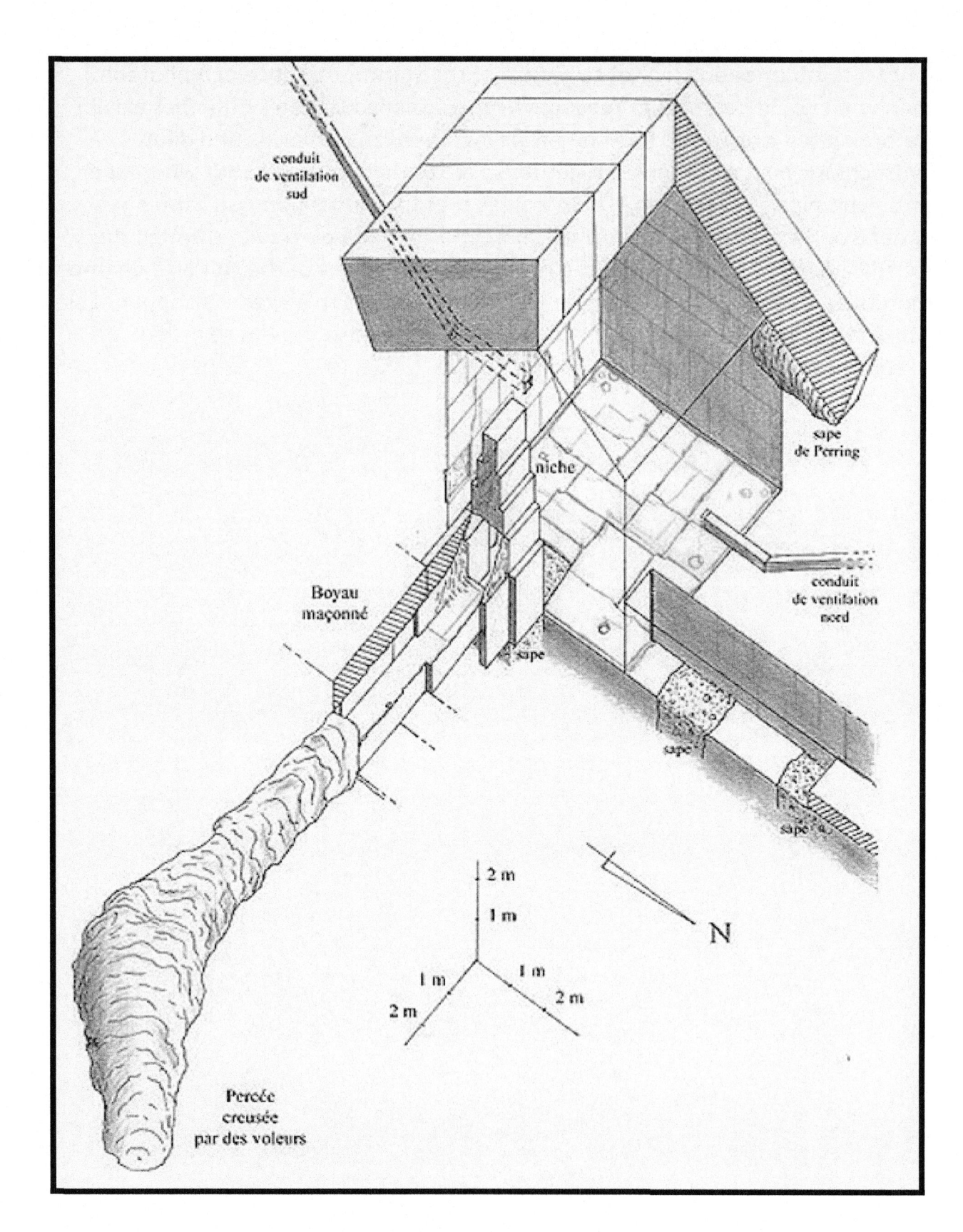

Schematic of the Queens Chamber

In 1993 German engineer Rudolph Gantenbrink sent a robot called Upuaut2 ("the opener of the ways") to video the inner walls of the shafts. He discovered that the southern shaft ended with a small Tura limestone slab in which two heavily corroded pieces of copper had been inserted. The door is estimated to be about six centimetres thick and is only about six meters from the outer surface of the pyramid. He tried to video the northern shaft, but couldn´t get around the curve. In 2002, a National Geographic robot, inserted a miniature fibre-optic camera into a three-quarter-of-an-inch hole to reveal a rough-hewn blocking stone about 21 centimetres beyond the original southern shaft door. It looks as if it is covering something, and there are cracks all over its surface. Shortly after, a robot built by iRobot of Boston made it up the north shaft, only to discover a door just like that of the southern shaft. (58)

End of one of the Queens Camber shafts

According to Dunn, hydrogen gas and spent chemicals flowed down the Queen's Chamber Passage toward its intersection with the bottom part of the Grand Gallery. There, the hydrogen gas passed through perforations in the bridging slab and travelled up the Grand Gallery, while the spent chemicals drained off into a large hole, 28 inches square, at the bottom of the west wall of the Gallery. Dunn claims that it filled the Grand Gallery and travelled into the King's Chamber, where it was used to create microwave energy. To this end, it was necessary to excite the hydrogen atoms by means of acoustic and electromagnetic (piezoelectric) energy.

The Grand Gallery continues the slope of the Ascending Passage, but is 8.6 m (28 ft) high and 46.68 m (153.1 ft) long. At the base it is 2.06 m (6.8 ft) wide, but after 2.29 m (7.5 ft) the blocks of stone in the walls are corbelled inwards by 7.6 cm (3.0 in) on each side. There are seven of these steps, so at the top the Grand Gallery is only 1.04 m (3.4 ft) wide. It is roofed by slabs of stone laid at a slightly steeper angle than the floor of the gallery, so that each stone fits into a slot cut in the top of the gallery like the teeth of a ratchet. The purpose may have been to have each block supported by the wall of the Gallery rather than resting on the block beneath it, which would have resulted in an unacceptable cumulative pressure at the lower end of the Gallery.

Granite splendor inside the Grand Gallery

According to Chris Dunn details of the Grand Gallery are extremely important and have no parallel in any other structure on Earth. Its geometric design predicts that sound originating within its space is focused through a passageway past the Antechamber and into the granite complex known as the King's Chamber. This phenomenon has been noted by musicians, acoustical engineers, military scientist and laypeople alike. Acoustic energy is the key to Dunn's hypothesis. One of the most interesting ideas in his book is that the Pyramid was coupled acoustically with the Earth and resonated in harmony with it. He makes a strong case that the King's Chamber in particular was designed to resonate at certain frequencies, hence the granite beams in its tower like superstructure and the nodular design of its floor. The purpose of this, according to Dunn, was to generate piezoelectric energy from the quartz bearing granite of which the chamber was made. Dunn also explains the unique design of the Grand Gallery, which the vibrations of the Earth were of insufficient amplitude to drive directly the granite beams above the King's Chamber. The purpose of the Gallery, he surmises, was to collect the vibrational energy over a large area and direct it into the King's Chamber, in the form of airborne sound, to increase the acoustic energy to the required level. What Dunn discovered, much to his amazement and counter to the common belief of Egyptologists was that most of the Grand Gallery is granite, and not limestone.

These are Chris Dunn's words:

In all the literature I had read, the Grand Gallery is described as being constructed of limestone. But here I was looking at granite! I noted a transition point further down the gallery where it changed from limestone to granite. I scanned the ceiling and saw, instead of the rough crumbling limestone one sees when first entering the gallery, what appeared to be, from 28 feet below, smooth highly polished granite. This was highly significant to me. It made sense that the material closer to the power center would be constructed of a material that was more resistant to heat. (59)

Dunn also claims that the Gallery was fitted with twenty-seven sets of Helmholtz resonators, fixed into position by means of the twenty, seven pairs of niches in the side ramps and the pair of grooves in the side walls. Helmholtz resonance is the phenomenon of air resonance in a cavity, such as when one blows across the top of an empty bottle. The name comes from a device created in the 1850s by

Hermann von Helmholtz, the "Helmholtz resonator", which he, the author of the classic study of acoustic science, used to identify the various frequencies or musical pitches present in music and other complex sounds. (60) Of course there are no signs of any resonators in the Great Pyramid at this time, or parts of them, so it is presumed that they were removed in the distant past, perhaps by the first Arabs that entered the pyramid. Being unable to use them for their original purpose, they most likely would have been recycled for their metal components.

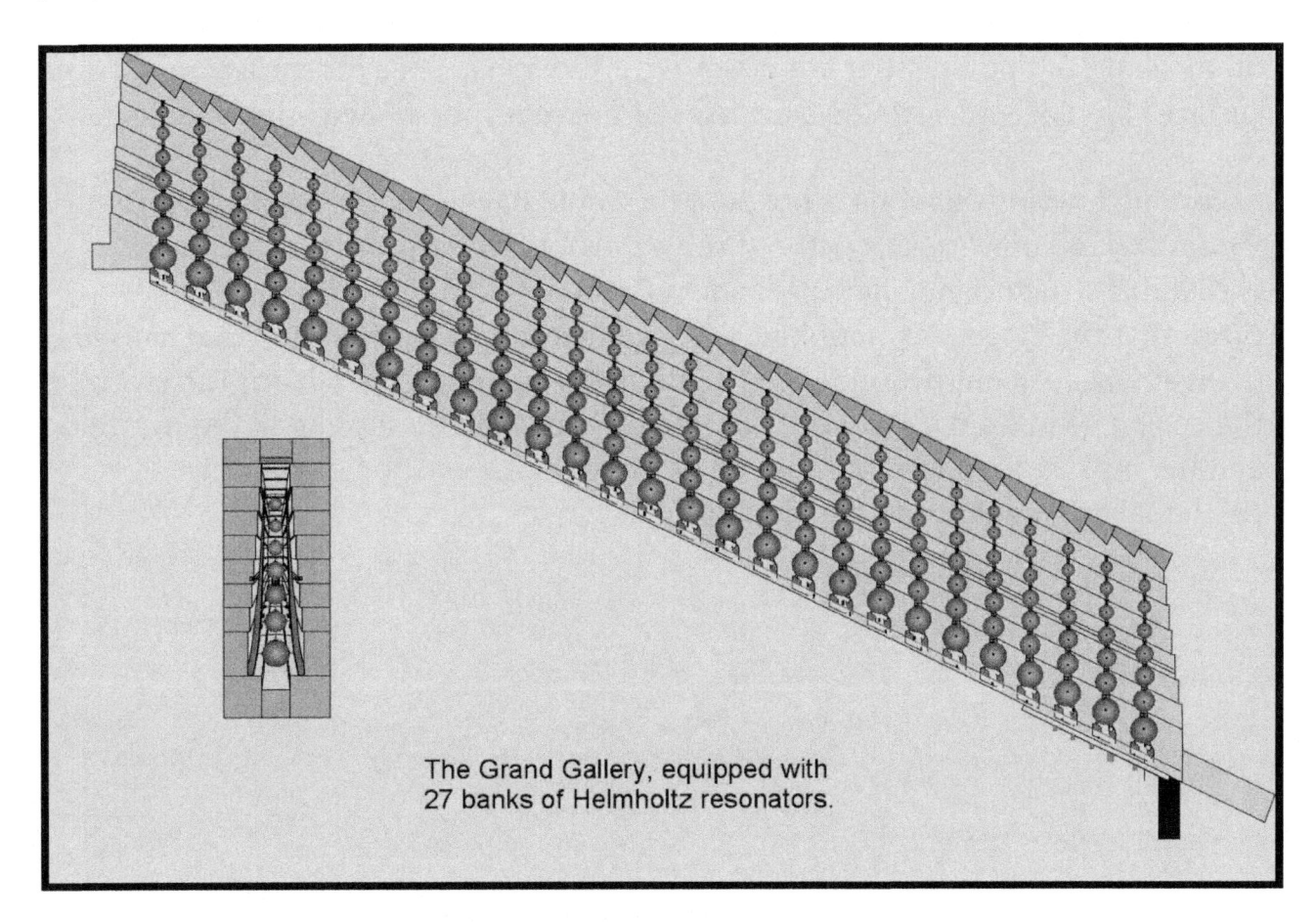

The Grand Gallery, equipped with 27 banks of Helmholtz resonators.

Schematic by engineer Chris Dunn

The King's Chamber is 10.47 m (34.4 ft) from east to west and 5.234 m (17.17 ft) north to south. It has a flat roof 5.974 m (19.60 ft) above the floor. 0.91 m (3.0 ft) above the floor there are two narrow shafts in the north and south walls (one is now filled by an extractor fan in an attempt to circulate air inside the pyramid). The purpose of these shafts is not clear: they appear to be aligned toward stars or areas of the northern and southern skies, yet one of them follows a dog-leg course through the masonry, indicating no intention to directly sight stars through them. They were long believed by Egyptologists to be "air shafts" for ventilation, but this idea has now been widely abandoned in favour of the shafts serving a ritualistic purpose associated with the ascension of the king's spirit to the heavens. (61) This of course is pure speculation.

The entire interior of the King's Chamber is lined in granite, supposedly from Aswan. The reasoning behind the use of this material rather than simply using limestone according to some Egyptologists was because it was the tomb of a pharaoh, and thus should be made of fine material. Why there are no inscriptions on the walls of this chamber are of course interesting, since most royal burial area surfaces are covered with the successes of the regal personage entombed.

According to Chris Dunn, he is not sure he would have considered that the Great Pyramid was a power plant without the evidence of energy affecting change within this structure. Reading in Flinders Petrie's *Pyramids and Temples of Gizeh* that the King's Chamber had been subject to a powerful force that caused the walls to push out over one inch made him sit up and take notice. The cracks in the ceiling beams did not seem, Dunn, to be explained by settling of the pyramid, and the historical explanation that all of this damage was the result of an earthquake just didn't seem to add up.

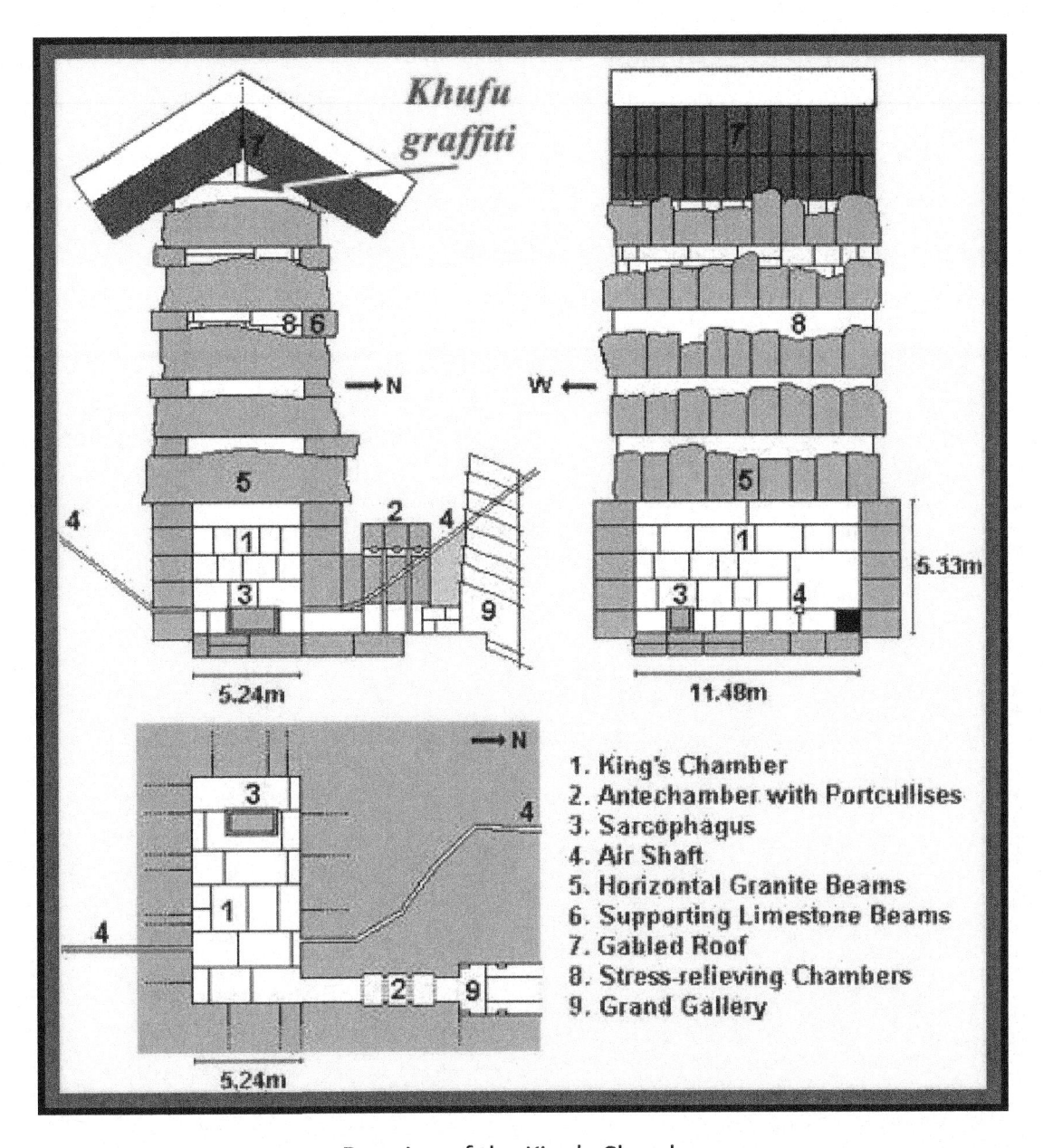

Drawing of the King's Chamber

The earthquake hypothesis according to Dunn simply doesn't work considering there is no similar damage in the lower parts of the Great Pyramid. Flinders Petrie surveyed the Descending Passage and found an amazing accuracy of .020 inch over 150 ft and a mere .250 inch over 350 ft of its constructed and excavated parts. With this evidence, there is no indication that the building had been shook to such a great extent that a chamber 175 ft above the bedrock would be significantly moved. Additionally, one might question why an earthquake would cause a chamber to expand rather than collapse? Combined, this point and the lack of supportive evidence in the lower parts of the Great Pyramid actually argue against and dismiss the earthquake theory. Faced with this evidence, and for a variety of other reasons he brings out in more detail in *The Giza Power Plant*, Dunn speculated that there had been an explosion in the King's Chamber. He had also speculated that this explosion resulted in a conflagration in the Grand Gallery that destroyed the proposed resonators in the Grand Gallery.

Rose granite box inside the King's Chamber

The only object present in the King's Chamber is a large granite box, presumed by most Egyptologists as being the sarcophagus created for pharaoh Khufu. However, of course his body was not found in the box, nor was there any sign of a lid. The sarcophagus is slightly larger than the Ascending Passage, which indicates that it must have been placed in the Chamber before the roof was put in place. Unlike the fine masonry of the walls of the Chamber, the sarcophagus is roughly finished, with saw marks visible in several places. This is in contrast with the finely finished and decorated sarcophagi found in other pyramids of the same period, and the smoothness of the walls in the King's Chamber. Petrie suggested that such a sarcophagus was intended but was lost in the river on the way north from Aswan and a hurriedly made replacement was used instead. However, this is pure speculation.

As regards the present dark appearance of the so called sarcophagus:

If subjected to excessive levels of energy, what changes would take place in an object like the coffer? Perhaps the coffer was originally red and quarried at the same time, in the same place, as the rest of the granite. Depending on other elements that were present at the time of the malfunction of the power plant, it is conceivable that certain changes would be recorded in any object fortunate enough to survive the accident. The comparatively thin sides and base of the coffer would naturally be more susceptible to excessive energy levels than would the huge granite blocks comprising the walls and ceiling. It could be suggested, therefore, that the coffer, without the ability to conduct the heat to which it was subjected, simply over-cooked, with a change in color being the result.

Above the roof of the King's Chamber, which is formed of nine slabs of stone weighing in total about 400 tons, are five compartments known as Relieving Chambers. The first four, like the King's Chamber, have flat roofs formed by the floor of the chamber above, but the final chamber has a pointed roof. Vyse suspected the presence of upper chambers when he found that he could push a long reed through a crack in the ceiling of the first chamber. From lower to upper, the chambers are known as "Davison's Chamber", "Wellington's Chamber", "Nelson's Chamber", "Lady Arbuthnot's Chamber", and "Campbell's Chamber". It is believed by many scholars that the compartments were intended to safeguard the King's Chamber from the possibility of a roof collapsing under the weight of stone above the Chamber. As the chambers were not intended to be seen, Egyptologists contend they were not finished in any way and a few of the stones still retain masons' marks painted on them. One of the stones in Campbell's

Chamber bears a mark, apparently the name of a work gang, which incorporates the only reference in the pyramid to Pharaoh Khufu. (62)

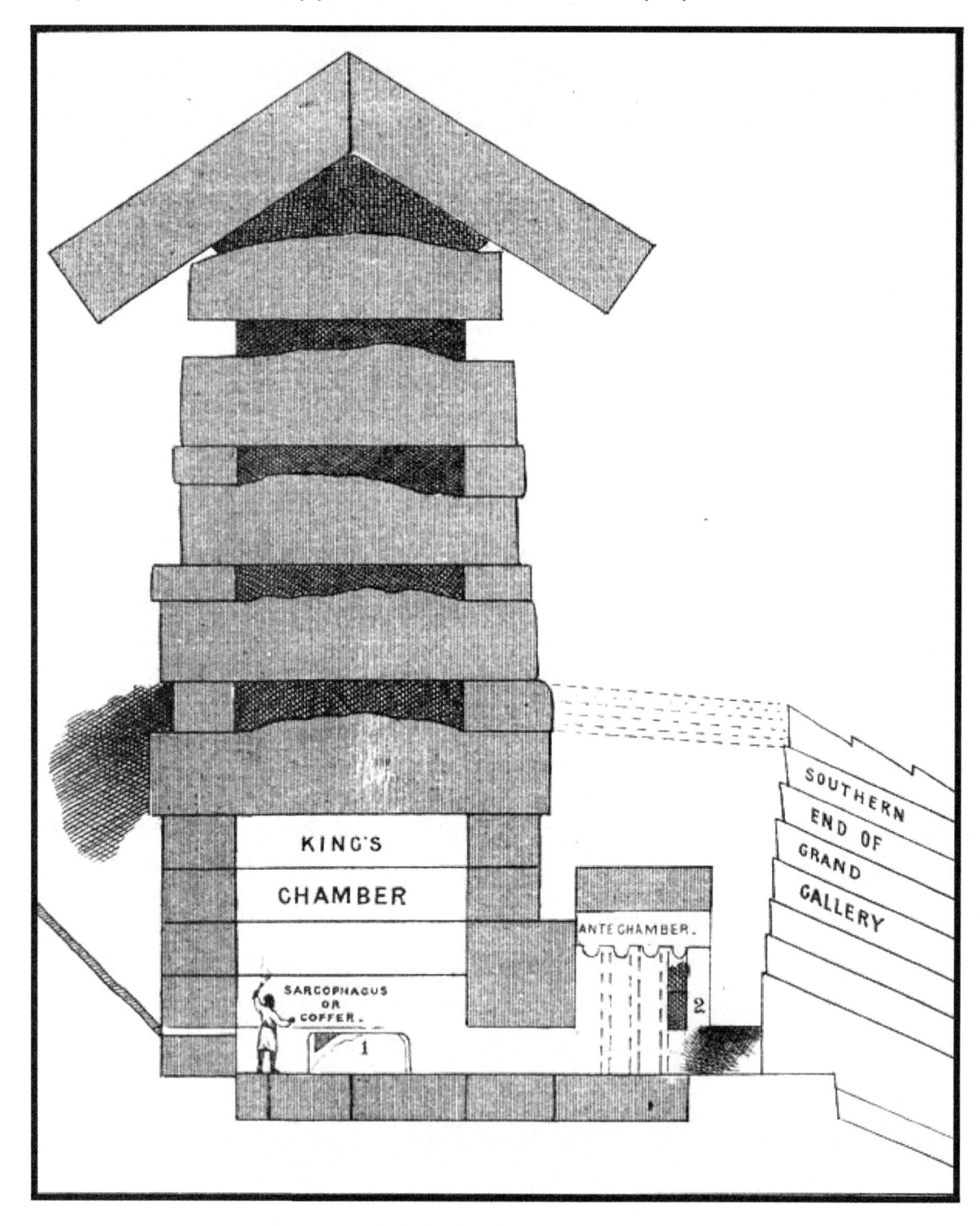

Simple drawing of the King's Chamber

Again, according to the work of Chris Dunn, whose very practical look at what the original function of the Great Pyramid could have been, this is what he says as regards the function of the Relieving Chambers:

Above the King's Chamber are five rows of granite beams, making a total of 43 beams weighing up to 70 tons each. Each layer is separated by a space large enough to crawl into. The red granite beams are cut square and parallel on three sides but were left seemingly untouched on the top surface, which was rough and uneven. Some of them even had holes gouged into the top of them. In cutting these giant monoliths, the builders evidently found it necessary to treat the beams destined for the uppermost chamber with the same respect as those intended for the ceiling directly above the King's Chamber. Each beam was cut flat and square on three sides, with the topside seemingly untouched. This is interesting, considering that the ones directly above the King's Chamber would be the only ones visible to those entering the pyramid. Even so, the attention these granite-ceiling beams received was nonetheless inferior to the attention commanded by the granite out of which the walls were constructed. (63)

He then goes on to say, in the same article:

To include so many monolithic blocks of granite in the structure is redundant. Especially when we consider the amount of incredibly difficult work that must have been invested in quarrying, cutting, transporting them 500 miles from the Aswan quarries, and then raising them to the 175 foot level of the pyramid. There is surely another reason for such an enormous effort and investment of time. And look at the characteristics of these beams. Why cut them square and flat on three sides and leave them rough on the top? If no one is going to look at them, why not make them rough on all sides? Better still; why not make all sides flat! It would certainly make it easier to assemble them!

The 43 giant beams above the King's Chamber were not included in the structure to relieve the King's Chamber from excessive pressure from above, but were included to fulfill a more advanced purpose. A simple yet refined technology can be discerned in the granite complex at the heart of the Great Pyramid, and with this technology the ancient power plant operated. The giant granite beams above the King's Chamber could be considered to be 43 individual bridges. Like the Tacoma Narrows Bridge, each one is capable of vibrating if a suitable type and amount of energy is introduced. If we were to concentrate on forcing just one of the beams to oscillate, with each of the other beams tuned to that frequency or a harmonic of that frequency, the other beams would be forced to vibrate at the same frequency or a harmonic.

If the energy contained within the forcing frequency was great enough, this transfer of energy from one beam to the next could affect the entire series of beams. A situation could exist, therefore, in which one individual beam in the ceiling directly above the King's Chamber could indirectly influence another beam in the uppermost chamber by forcing it to vibrate at the same frequency as the original forcing frequency or one of its harmonic frequencies.

The amount of energy absorbed by these beams from the source would depend on the natural resonant frequency of the beam. The ability of the beams to dissipate the energy they are subject to would have to be considered, as well as the natural resonating frequency of the granite beam. If the forcing frequency (sound input) coincided with the natural frequency of the beam, and there was little damping (the beams were not restrained from vibrating), then the transfer of energy would be maximized. Consequently, so would the vibration of the beams.

It is quite clear that the giant granite beams above the King's Chamber have a length of 17 feet (the width of the Chamber) in which they can react to induced motion and vibrate without restraint. Some damping may occur if the beams adjacent faces are so close that they rub together. However, if the beams vibrate in unison, it is possible that such damping would not happen. To perfect the ability of the 43 granite beams to resonate with the forcing frequency, the natural frequency of each beam would have to be of the same frequency as the forcing frequency, or be in harmony with it. It would be possible to tune a length of granite, such as those found in the Great Pyramid, by altering its physical dimensions.

A precise frequency could be attained by either altering the length of the beam, which is allowed to vibrate (as in the playing of stringed instruments), or by removing material from the beam's mass, as in the tuning of bells. (A bell is tuned to a fundamental hum and its harmonics by removing metal from critical areas.)

Striking it while it was being held in a position similar to that of the beams above the King's Chamber, as one would strike a tuning fork, could induce oscillation of the beam. The frequency of the vibration would be sampled and more material removed until the correct frequency had been reached. Rather than a lack of attention, therefore, the top surfaces of these granite beams may have arrived at their present shape through the application of more careful attention and work than the sides or the bottom. Before being placed inside the Great Pyramid, each beam may have been suspended on each end in the same position that it would hold once placed inside the Great Pyramid, and a considerable amount of attention paid to the upper surface.

The granite complex inside the Great Pyramid, therefore, is poised ready to convert vibrations from the earth into electricity. What is lacking is a sufficient amount of energy to drive the beams and activate the piezoelectric properties within. The ancients, though, had anticipated the need for more energy than what would be collected only within the King's Chamber. They had determined that they needed to tap into the vibrations of the earth over a larger area inside the pyramid and deliver that energy to the power center, the King's Chamber thereby substantially increasing the amplitude of the oscillations of the granite.

While modern research into architectural acoustics might predominantly focus upon minimizing the reverberation effects of sound in enclosed spaces, there is reason to believe that the ancient pyramid builders were attempting to achieve the opposite. The Grand Gallery, which is considered to be an architectural masterpiece, is an enclosed space in which resonators were installed in the slots along the ledge that runs the length of the Gallery. As the earth's vibration flowed through the Great Pyramid, the resonators converted the energy to airborne sound. By design, the angles and surfaces of the walls and ceiling of the Grand Gallery, caused reflection of the sound and its focus into the King's Chamber.

Although the King's Chamber was also responding to the energy flowing through the pyramid, much of the energy would flow past it. The design and utility of the Grand Gallery was to transfer the energy flowing through a large area of the pyramid into the resonant King's Chamber. This sound was then focused into the granite resonating cavity at sufficient amplitude to drive the granite ceiling beams to oscillation. These beams, in turn, compelled the beams above them to resonate in harmonic sympathy. Thus, the input of sound and the maximization of resonance, the entire granite complex, in effect, became a vibrating mass of energy.

The question of what the energy was actually used for, and to this Dunn does not go into much speculation. His basic theory is that the Great Pyramid was a geomechanical power plant that responded sympathetically with the earth's vibrations and converted that energy into electricity. They used the electricity to power their civilization, he believes, which included machine tools with which they shaped hard igneous rock. (64) Other theories have suggested that the Great Pyramid was a nuclear power plant, weapon of some sort able to shoot focused energy at flying objects or into space, a sacred metaphysical structure of initiation, etc. I leave it to the reader to explore such avenues, as there are too many to put into a book like this.

The other major object on the Giza plateau which has perplexed people for centuries, at least is of course the Sphinx. It is not known by what name the creators called their statue, as the Great Sphinx does not appear in any known inscription of the Old Kingdom, and there are no inscriptions anywhere describing its construction or its original purpose. In the New Kingdom, the Sphinx was called *Hor-em-akhet* (English: Horus of the Horizon; Hellenized: *Harmachis*), and the pharaoh Thutmose IV (1401–1391 or 1397–1388 BC) (65) specifically referred to it as such in his Dream Stele. The commonly used name *Sphinx* was given to it in classical antiquity, about 2000 years after the accepted date of its construction, by reference to a Greek mythological beast with a lion's body, a woman's head and the wings of an eagle. According to Stephen Mehler and the Khemit School, the original name of the Sphinx is *Tefnut,* "the Great Mother" and is 54,000 years old.

Great Sphinx in its enclosure

Despite conflicting evidence and viewpoints over the years, the view held by modern Egyptology at large remains that the Great Sphinx was built in approximately 2500 BC for the pharaoh Khafre, the proposed builder of the Second Pyramid at Giza. (66) Selim Hassan, writing in 1949 on recent excavations of the Sphinx enclosure, summed up the problem:

"Taking all things into consideration, it seems that we must give the credit of erecting this, the world's most wonderful statue, to Khafre, but always with this reservation: that there is not one single contemporary inscription which connects the Sphinx with Khafre; so, sound as it may appear, we must treat the evidence as

circumstantial, until such time as a lucky turn of the spade of the excavator will reveal to the world a definite reference to the erection of the Sphinx." (67)

The Dream Stele, erected much later by the pharaoh Thutmose IV, associates the Sphinx with Khafre. When the stele was discovered, its lines of text were already damaged and incomplete, and only referred to *Khaf*, not Khafre. An extract which was translated states:

"... which we bring for him: oxen...and all the young vegetables; and we shall give praise to *Wenofer*... *Khaf*...the statue made for *Atum-Hor-em-Akhet*."

The Egyptologist Thomas Young, finding the *Khaf* hieroglyphs in a damaged cartouche used to surround a royal name, inserted the glyph *re* to complete Khafre's name. When the Stele was re-excavated in 1925, the lines of text referring to *Khaf* flaked off and were destroyed. As the actual hard evidence that the Sphinx was built during the time of Khafre is basically non-existent, and that circumstantial associations such as the discovery nearby of a diorite statue presumed to be that of Khafre, found buried upside down along with other debris in the nearby Valley Temple, other dates and ideas have emerged.

Sphinx and the Dream Stela

In fact, some of the earliest of Egyptologists and other excavators of the Giza pyramid complex believed the Great Sphinx and other structures in the Sphinx enclosure predated the traditional date of construction. In 1857, for example, Auguste Mariette, founder of the Egyptian Museum in Cairo, unearthed the much later Inventory Stela (estimated to be from the 26th dynasty about 678 to 525 BC), which tells how Khufu came upon the Sphinx, already buried in sand. And Gaston Maspero, the French Egyptologist and second director of the Egyptian Museum in Cairo, conducted a survey of the Sphinx in 1886 and concluded:

"The Sphinx stela shows, in line thirteen, the cartouche of Khephren. I believe that to indicate an excavation carried out by that prince, following which, the almost certain proof that the Sphinx was already buried in sand by the time of Khafre and his predecessors."

Then we have Colin Reader, an English geologist who independently conducted a more recent survey of the enclosure, agrees that the various quarries on the site have been excavated around the Sphinx Causeway. Because these quarries are known to have been used by Khufu, Reader concludes that the Causeway (and the temples on either end thereof) must predate Khufu, thereby casting doubt on the conventional Egyptian chronology. (68) And quite possibly the most scientific explanation of how old the Sphinx could be is from the work of Boston University geologist Robert Schoch.

Photos of the Sphinx from the 1860s

The Sphinx water erosion hypothesis contends that the main type of weathering evident on the enclosure walls of the Great Sphinx was caused by prolonged and extensive rainfall. R. A. Schwaller de Lubicz, a French alternative Egyptologist, first claimed evidence of water erosion on the walls of the Sphinx enclosure in the 1950s. (69) John Anthony West, an author and alternative Egyptologist, investigated Schwaller de Lubicz's ideas further and, in 1989, sought the opinion of Robert Schoch. In Schoch's own words:

"In 1990 I first traveled to Egypt, with the sole purpose of examining the Great Sphinx from a geological perspective. I assumed that the Egyptologists were correct in their dating, but soon I discovered that the geological evidence was not compatible with what the Egyptologists were saying. On the body of the Sphinx, and on the walls of the Sphinx Enclosure (the pit or

hollow remaining after the Sphinx's body was carved from the bedrock), I found heavy erosional features (seen in the accompanying photographs) that I concluded could only have been caused by rainfall and water runoff. The thing is, the Sphinx sits on the edge of the Sahara Desert and the region has been quite arid for the last 5000 years. Furthermore, various structures securely dated to the Old Kingdom show only erosion that was caused by wind and sand (very distinct from the water erosion). To make a long story short, I came to the conclusion that the oldest portions of the Great Sphinx, what I refer to as the core-body, must date back to an earlier period (at least 5000 B.C., and maybe as early as 7000 or 9000 B.C.), a time when the climate was very different and included more rain." (70)

Detail of Sphinx showing repair work

Schoch further notes the same heavy precipitation-induced weathering as seen on the walls of the Sphinx enclosure is also found on the core blocks of the Sphinx and Valley Temples, both known to have been originally constructed from blocks taken from the Sphinx enclosure when the body was carved. Though the presence of extensive 4th Dynasty repair work to the Sphinx and associated temples is acknowledged by such Egyptologists as Lehner and Hawass, Schoch contends:

"Therefore if the granite facing is covering deeply weathered limestone, the original limestone structures must predate by a considerable degree the granite facing. Obviously, if the limestone cores (originating from the Sphinx ditch) of the temples predate the granite ashlars (granite facings), and the granite ashlars are attributable to Khafre of the Fourth Dynasty, then the Great Sphinx was built prior to the reign of Khafre." (71)

Weathering of Sphinx enclosure on the left of the photo

Note that Schoch says that the granite ashlars are "attributed to Khafre.) We will cover the Valley Temple and adjacent Sphinx Temple a little later.

The Sphinx itself is heavily weathered, and repairs having being going on supposedly from the Old Kingdom up to present day. The head is in remarkable condition as compared to the body, and here Robert Schoch explains why this is the case:

"Many people have said to me that the Great Sphinx cannot be so old, in part because the head is clearly a dynastic Egyptian head and the dynastic period did not start until about 3000 B.C. In fact, if you look at the current Great Sphinx you may notice that the head is actually too small for the body. It is clear to me that the current head is not the original head. The original head would have become severely weathered and eroded. It was later re-carved, during dynastic times, and in the re-carving it naturally became smaller. Thus, the head of the Great Sphinx is not the original head. In fact, the Sphinx may not have originally been a sphinx at all. Perhaps it was a male lion."

Head of the Sphinx clearly seems to have been recarved

The other two major structures associated with, and in front of the Sphinx are the so called Sphinx Temple and Valley Temple. As previously stated, the enormous limestone blocks that make up both of these were extracted from the Sphinx enclosure in the process of the Sphinx's creation. Some of the blocks weigh an estimated 100 tons, or perhaps even more, so if the dynastic Egyptians were responsible for this work, what tools would they have had to be able to cut out such massive stones?

Some believe that the Sphinx was originally just the rough form of a head rising above the plateau, called a yardang by geologists prior to its actual fully sculpted form. Yardangs become elongated features typically three or more times longer than wide and when viewed from above, often resembling the hull of a boat. Facing the wind is a steep, blunt face that gradually gets lower and narrower toward the lee end. Yardangs are formed by wind erosion, typically of an originally flat surface formed from areas of harder and softer material. The soft material is eroded and removed by the wind, and the harder material remains. If Robert Schoch's theory is correct, in that the weathering of the Sphinx is thousands of years older than the time of Khufu and Khafre, then clearly the shaping of it occurred earlier, and if this is the case, then both the Sphinx and Valley Temples are also thousands of years older than these dynastic Egyptians.

Interior of the heavily plundered Sphinx Temple

The condition of the Sphinx Temple is far poorer than that of the Valley Temple, not meaning that one is older than the other, but that the Sphinx Temple was much more of a victim of plundering for its building materials. Both Yousef Awyan and Stephen Mehler believe, and I concur on our April 2014 exploration of the area that both temples are of the same vintage. It could be that the Valley Temple, at least its granite core was spared as it was buried in sand for a prolonged period of time, up until the 19th century. (72) If the interior of the Sphinx Temple was anything like how the Valley Temple still looks, massive square granite columns and horizontal cross beams would have been in place, the stone most likely having come from Aswan.

Also, the interior and exterior of the walls most likely had Aswan granite facing, not simply applied to the limestone surface but bonded in a three dimensional matrix. On one of the interior blocks of the Valley temple Chris Dunn measured its surface smoothness, which appeared to be 2/10,000 of an inch from being laser perfect, a feat that the dynastic Egyptians most likely could not achieve. So rather than in fact having anything to do with the construction of either the Sphinx or Valley temples, the pharaohs may simply have inherited them, and used them for their own purposes.

Chris Dunn measuring inside the Valley Temple

Rose granite facing stones in the Valley temple

The photo above shows the extreme weathering of the interior of the Valley Temple's granite megalithic blocks. The interior pillars once supported a roof of which only the primary granite beams remain. There are six pillars in the north-south segment of the chamber, and two rows of five pillars in the east-west segment. The wall facing of granite is cut and fitted with extreme precision, with odd shapes that give the appearance of a 3D jigsaw puzzle. Some of the facing stones are shaped so intricately as to have three or more exposed surfaces and multiple corners and angles.

Massive granite columns in the Valley Temple

Yousef Awyan outside the Valley Temple

Being concealed within the desert sands spared the Valley temple from having its alabaster flooring and granite facing being stripped away for other uses, allowing us a glimpse of the artistry and engineering of the mighty builders. Although it may lack the cosmetic flourishes of the temples of later dynasties, its construction is vastly superior to later Old Kingdom structures.

And again, why would that be? Why would the later builders' work be at least technically inferior and clearly less challenging from that which preceded them? As far as I know Egyptologists have no logical answer for this, and possibly the most intriguing aspect about the Giza Plateau is not really addressed at all by them; the tunnels and shafts.

Many readers will have heard about the possibility that there are rooms and perhaps tunnels under the Sphinx, and the famous psychic Edgar Casey stated that in fact some sort of "hall of records" would eventually be found there. This has led to wild speculations about connections with Atlantean civilizations, and even the presence of ancient aliens, but what is the actual evidence?

I was very privileged in both 2013 and 2014 to go beyond the well-worn paths trod by tourists, and venture into areas of the Giza Plateau that most people ever see, thanks to Yousef Awyan. As we walked past the Sphinx and towards the Great Pyramids, we encountered several shafts of substantial width and breadth which were cut deep into the bedrock, and since the sands of time had largely filled them up, it was impossible to see how deep they originally went, and to where.

The author filming at one of the shafts with Sphinx head in behind

View looking down into one of the shafts

Yousef stated that the shafts connected with tunnels traveling east to west and north to south, and this whole system was created to carry water from the ancient Nile, called the *Ur Nil* to the Giza Plateau and that this was the water used in the energy processes of the pyramids. He said that there were at least three levels of tunnels, and proceeded to guide me into them.

In the labyrinth of the first level

The first level is somewhat open above, as seen in the photo above. But through a series of labyrinthine passages level one leads to vertical and angled shafts which lead to level two.

Just a few of the many entrances into the tunnel and shaft system

Some of these shafts were clearly used by the dynastic Egyptians as tombs, but just because they used them does not mean that they carved them out of the solid limestone bedrock. The tombs are clearly what Yousef calls "site transformation" which is a very apt term.

Sculpted bedrock surfaces that few visitors ever see

The author inspecting the water weathering in level 2

We went into many sections of the second level, and saw clear signs of erosion, which appeared to have been done by water. The windblown sand of the plateau could not have entered these underground areas. Unfortunately the system of these tunnels and shafts are so vast and complex that we were only able to see a tiny fraction of what is still present, but future trips there, every spring for the rest of my life should lead to the gathering of my evidence.

Hopefully the photos and other evidence presented in this book shows you that the dynastic Egyptians did not have the tools required to shape granite, basalt, diorite, quartzite or other hard stones, at least not to the level of finish we see in the Valley Temple, interior of the Great Pyramids, Osirion, and obelisks for example. Nor were they likely to have cut the tunnel systems, including the descending passage in the Great Pyramid. It therefore seems quite clear that these were not the works of the pharaohs, but were an inheritance from an older culture, called by Stephen Mehler, Yousef Awyan and others the Khemitians. The

Colossi of Memnon for example would most likely be in their original places due to their massive scale, whereas obelisks, statuary, columns and casing stones could have been moved by the dynastic Egyptians with a large enough work force.

What we can tell by the sometimes vicious nature of some of the pharaohs was that they would deface statues of earlier rulers, eradicate their hieroglyphics from walls, so why, with such disdain, can we not entertain the idea that they recycled some of the hard stone works that may be even far older? If you have contempt or disregard for some of those that came before, what would you care about the accomplishments of people beyond the scope of written records, oral traditions or even memory?

I would follow my brother Yousef anywhere

The simple considerations to ponder over after having looked at the evidence in this book are as follows. If the dynastic Egyptians coalesced as a distinct society around 3100 BC, then why were most of their greatest accomplishments, such as the works on the Giza Plateau made a scant 600 years later, and never replicated or bettered? To state that it was a lack of resources or wealth would be a very cheap and easy way of not addressing this question. And why is it these amazing works also lack inscriptions, or if they do, such as some of the boxes inside the Serapeum at Saqqara, why are the hieroglyphs far inferior to the stone surfaces themselves? It is most likely because the inscriptions were made later in time, by people who did not have the capability to produce the original pieces.

What we have seen is that, in general it has been people outside of Egyptology, such as engineers, stone masons, geologists and people of other disciplines that have asked the penetrating questions probed in this book. In some cases their enquiries and insights have been met with not only opposition, but ridicule from academics in the Egyptology field, who frankly have poor counter arguments at best. One of the most classic cases is that where Zahi Hawass, when presented the evidence by John Anthony West and Robert Schoch of the weathering of the Sphinx and the implications that it could be much older than the dynastic Egyptians stated "no single artifact, no single inscription, or pottery, or anything has been found until now, in any place to predate the Egyptian civilization more than 5,000 years ago." (73)

Does he not regard the works themselves as the evidence? We are clearly at a point in time where the knowledge of a relatively small group of specialized academics is not sufficient to answer all of the questions that book looks at. The only way that the truth about how ancient the masterworks of Egypt are, is through a very a multidisciplinary approach. In the words of Abd'El Hakim Awyan, the guide who was born across the street from the Sphinx, held two university degrees, and spent most of his life in the field observing, as well as consulting with the elders that take care of the ancient sites of Egypt (paraphrasing): 'open your eyes!'

16/ Bibliography

1/ Siliotti, Alberto (1998). *The Discovery of Ancient Egypt*. Edison, New Jersey: Book Sales, Inc. ISBN 0-7858-1360-8.

2/ Murray, S. A., (2009). The library: An illustrated history. New York: Skyhorse Publishing, p.17

3/ Murray, S. (2009). *The library: An illustrated history*. Chicago, IL: Skyhorse Publishing, (pp. 15).

4/ http://realhistoryww.com/world_history/ancient/Egypt_4.htm

5/ Hall Jonathan M. (2007). *A History of the Archaic Greek World, ca. 1200-479 BCE*. Wiley-Blackwell. ISBN 978-0-631-22667-3.

6/ "The Fall of the Egyptian Old Kingdom". BBC. 17 February 2011.

7/ "The Kushite Conquest of Egypt". Ancientsudan.org.

8/ Dr. Okasha El Daly (2005), *Egyptology: The Missing Millennium: Ancient Egypt in Medieval Arabic Writings,* UCL Press, ISBN 1-84472-063-2.

9/ Edward Chaney, "Roma Britannica and the Cultural Memory of Egypt: Lord Arundel and the Obelisk of Domitian", in Roma Britannica: Art Patronage and Cultural Exchange in Eighteenth-Century Rome, eds. D. Marshall, K. Wolfe and S. Russell, British School at Rome, 2011, pp. 147–70.

10/ Suʿād Māhir (1966). *Muhafazat Al Gumhuriya Al Arabiya Al Mutaheda wa Asaraha al baqiah fi al asr al islamim*. Majlis al-Aʿlá lil-Shuʾūn al-Islāmīyah.

11/ Bard, Kathryn (1999). *Encyclopedia of the Archaeology of Ancient Egypt*. Routledge. p. 587. ISBN 978-0-415-18589-9.

14/ http://s8int.com/phile/page52.html

15/ Rehren T, et al, "5,000 years old Egyptian iron beads made from hammered meteoritic iron", Journal of Archaeological Science 2013 text.

16/ http://www.gizapyramid.com/stephenmehler1.htm

17/ Guy Lecuyot. "THE RAMESSEUM (EGYPT), RECENT ARCHAEOLOGICAL RESEARCH". Archéologies d'Orient et d'Occident.

18/ Arnold, Dieter (2003). Strudwick, Helen (ed), ed. *The encyclopaedia of ancient Egyptian architecture*. I.B.Tauris. p. 196. ISBN 1-86064-465-1.

19/ "The Seventy Wonders of the Ancient World", edited by Chris Scarre (1999) Thames & Hudson, London.

20/ Wolfgang Waitkus, *Die Texte in den unteren Krypten des Hathortempels von Dendera: ihre Aussagen zur Funktion und Bedeutung dieser Räume*, Mainz 1997 ISBN 3-8053-2322-0.

21/ Childress, D. H. (2000). Technology of the gods: the incredible sciences of the ancients. Kempton, Ill: Adventures Unlimited Press. ISBN 0932813739

22/ Stern, Bolko (1896 reprinted 1998). *Ägyptische Kulturgeschichte*. Reprint-Verlag-Leipzig. pp. 106–108. ISBN 978-3826219085.

23/ http://www.kch42.dial.pipex.com/egypttour_abydos.htm

24/ Rice, Michael (1999). *Who's Who in Ancient Egypt*. Routledge.

25/ Brand, Peter J. *The Monuments of Seti I: Epigraphic, Historical and Art Historical Analysis* Brill September 2000, ISBN 978-90-04-11770-9 p. 175

26/ Furlong, David The Osirion and the Flower of Life: Photographic evidence from the Osirion.

27/ Curran, B. A. (2009). *Obelisk: A history*. Cambridge, Mass: Burndy Library.

28/ de la Vergne, Jack (2003). *Hard Rock Miner's Handbook*. Tempe/North Bay: McIntosh Engineering. pp. 4–12. ISBN 0-9687006-1-6.

29/ Mendelssohn, Kurt (1974), *The Riddle of the Pyramids*, London: Thames & Hudson

30/ Krystek, Lee. "Venus in the Corner Pocket: The Controversial Theories of Immanuel Velikovsky". Museum of Unnatural Mystery.

31/ Burbridge, G. R. et al. "Evidence for the occurrence of violent events in the nuclei of galaxies." Reviews of Modern Physics 35 (1963): 947.

32/ Oort, J. H. "The Galactic Center." Annual Reviews of Astronomy & Astrophysics 15 (1977): 295.

33/ Lo, K. Y., and Claussen, M. J. "High-resolution observations of ionized gas in central 3 paresecs of the Galaxy: possible evidence for infall." Nature 306 (1983): 647.

34/ History Channel, *Ancient Egypt - Part 3: Greatest Pharaohs 3150 to 1351 BC*, History Channel, 1996.

35/ Lehner, Mark (1997). *The Complete Pyramids*. Thames and Hudson. ISBN 0-500-05084-8.

36/ Fernandez, I., J. Becker, S. Gillies. "Places: 796289136 (Saqqarah)". Pleiades.

37/ Mathieson, I., Bettles, E., Dittmer, J., & Reader, C. (1999). The National Museums of Scotland Saqqara survey project, earth sciences 1990-1998. *Journal of Egyptian archaeology*, *85*, 21-43.

38/ Dodson, A. (2000). The Eighteenth Century discovery of the Serapeum. *KMT*, *11*(3), 48-53.

39/ http://www.gizapower.com/Precision.htm

40/ http://science.howstuffworks.com/environmental/earth/geology/quartz-info.htm

41/ http://www.theglobaleducationproject.org/egypt/articles/hrdfact3.php

42/ http://voices.yahoo.com/did-ancient-egyptians-technology-far-beyond-the-8128896.html

43/ http://www.touregypt.net/featurestories/suntemples.htm

44/ http://depts.washington.edu/silkroad/texts/tafur.html#ch5

45/ Verner, Miroslav. The Pyramids: The Mystery, Culture, and Science of Egypt's Great Monuments. Grove Press. 2001 (1997). ISBN 0-8021-3935-3

46/ http://www.soulsofdistortion.nl/SODA_chapter8.html

47/ yubanet.com "Concrete Blocks Used in Great Pyramids Construction" Drexel University

48/ http://www.cmc-concrete.com/CMC%20Publications/2007,%20The%20Great%20Pyramid%20Debate,%2

49/ Romer, John (2007). *The Great Pyramid: Ancient Egypt Revisited*. Cambridge University Press. p. 41. ISBN 978-0-521-87166-2.

50/ http://www.cheops-pyramide.ch/khufu-pyramid/stone-quarries.html

51/ http://cassiopaea.org/forum/index.php?topic=27990.0

52/ Flinders Petrie, Willam: The Pyramids and Temples of Gizeh, 1883, p. 421

53/ Verner, Miroslav: The Pyramids, 2001, p. 195

54/ Isler, Martin: Journal of the American Research Center in Egypt, 20:1983, pp. 27-32

55/ Chamber". Public Broadcasting Service.

56/ http://www.newdawnmagazine.com/articles/a-new-theory-for-the-great-pyramid-how-science-is-changing-our-view-of-the-past

57/ http://www.newdawnmagazine.com/articles/a-new-theory-for-the-great-pyramid-how-science-is-changing-our-view-of-the-past

58/ http://www.ancientegyptonline.co.uk/queenschambergp.html

59/ www.gizapower.com: The Official Chris Dunn Website

60/ Helmholtz, Hermann von (1885), *On the sensations of tone as a physiological basis for the theory of music*, Second English Edition, translated by Alexander J. Ellis. London: Longmans, Green, and Co., p. 44.

61/ Jackson and Stamp (2002) Pyramid: Beyond Imagination. pp. 79 & 104

62/ Vyse, H. (1840) *Operations Carried on at the Pyramids of Gizeh in 1837: With an Account of a Voyage into Upper Egypt, and an Appendix. Vol I.* London: James Fraser, Regent Street.

63/ http://www.bibliotecapleyades.net/piramides/esp_piramide_14.htm

64/ http://www.gizapyramid.com/chrisdunn.htm

65/ http://en.wikipedia.org/wiki/Thutmose_IV#Dates_and_length_of_reign

66/ Christiane Zivie-Coche, *Sphinx: History of a Monument*, pages 99–100 (Cornell University Press, 2002). ISBN 0-8014-3962-0

67/ Hassan, Selim (1949). *The Sphinx: Its history in the light of recent excavations.* Cairo: Government Press, 1949.

68/ Reader, Colin (2002). "Giza Before the Fourth Dynasty", *Journal of the Ancient Chronology Forum*, 9 (2002), 5–21.

69/ R. A. Schwaller de Lubicz, *Sacred Science: The King of Pharaonic Theocracy* New York: Inner Traditions International, 1982. ISBN 0-89281-007-6

70/ http://www.robertschoch.com/sphinxcontent.html

71/ http://www.robertschoch.com/geodatasphinx.html

72/ http://www.bluffton.edu/~sullivanm/egypt/giza/pyramids/valtemp.html

73/ http://www.pbs.org/wgbh/nova/pyramid/explore/howold.html

Printed in Great Britain
by Amazon